D1488300

HIGH SCHOOL FOOTBALL

# POSITION POWER

BY JEFFREY STERN

## WORKING THE WINGS

FROM REFEREE AND THE NATIONAL ASSOCIATION OF SPORTS OFFICIALS

**High School Football**
**Position Power: Working the Wings**

By Jeffrey Stern, senior editor, Referee/NASO

Graphics and layout by Dustin Brown, graphic designer, Referee/NASO

Published by Referee Enterprises, Inc., and the National Association of Sports Officials.

Printed in the United States of America

ISBN-13: 978-1-58208-358-2

# Contents

# Introduction

**While** every position on a football officiating crew is important, I truly believe the wings are the heart and soul of the group. They are involved in virtually every play, from pre-snap to dead ball. And they have to listen to the commentary of the non-players on the sidelines.

Working the wings is a physical and mental challenge. There's a lot to know and remember.

I wish this book had been around when I was starting out as a wing official 40-some years ago. It would have made me a better official. But this is by no means a book for a newcomer. There's a lot of information between these covers so that even a veteran can learn a great deal.

I hope you get as much out of reading it as I did putting it together. It was truly a labor of love.

My deep appreciation to Referee graphic artist Dustin Brown, who laid out this book and added the illustrations. Some the passages were written by others. Many thanks to George Demetriou, Jerry Grunska and Jon Bible for their insights.

Jeffrey Stern
Senior editor
*Referee* magazine

# CHAPTER ONE

# 5 THINGS A WING MUST KNOW

"(The white area) is our domain — our office, if you will. We need that area to work in and it becomes a safety issue if players and coaches crowd up to the sideline."

— Retired NFL line judge Tom Barnes

**Every** position on an officiating crew is important. But most wing officials will tell you they have more going on than their crewmates.

Wing officials are involved in virtually every play. They count players, judge the legality of offensive formations, watch for presnap fouls and observe blocking. They may not have to more than a step to cover plays that end close to the previous spot, or bust downfield to cover a long gainer. And then there's the coaches to deal with.

It would be impossible to whittle down everything a wing official does in a few hundred words. Obviously, there's enough to do and think about that an entire book has been dedicated to the topic!

As a warm-up, here are five topics intended to get you into a wing official frame of mind. You'll find these topics covered in greater detail elsewhere in this book. But for now, keep these points in mind.

## Start at the sideline or wider.

If the ball is at the nearer hashmark or a wide receiver is positioned near your sideline, you'll benefit from being a few steps off the field. You are entitled to three yards of space between the sideline and the team area (often referred to as "the white" since many fields have that area painted solid white) in which to maneuver. Start with a cushion and maintain it during the play. You want to observe the play, not be part of it.

Before the game, you should stake your claim to the three-yard belt. The coaches know they can't be there from the time the snap is imminent until the ball is dead, but they'll creep up any chance they get. When you're working in the white, use all of it. The coaches won't have a choice but to be behind you.

Ascertain the name of the get-back coach, the assistant who will ensure players and coaches stay in the team area. The head linesman should instruct the chain crew to keep the chains at least a yard from the sideline.

The wider view will give a better perspective and more time to look. Also, you don't want to be part of the play. If you're backing up and trying to get out of the way, your priority becomes survival and your officiating will be less effective.

## Keep your distance.

As the play progresses, you must maintain distance and shuffle step downfield. Remain off the field and slightly behind the runner during your side shuffle. Keep your chest facing the field while sliding downfield with the runner. Once the runner crosses the line and breaks free of defenders, you can turn your hips and accelerate but trail him at a reasonable distance. Until the runner is contacted by an opponent, you must watch the players around the ball. Watch for illegal acts by players of both teams.

If the runner is forced out of bounds, stop and let him pass in front of you. Then turn toward the players out of bounds as you give the stop-the-clock signal. Keep your eyes on players; if you stare at the spot, you'll miss late hits. Your foot is all you need to mark the spot. Don't drop a beanbag unless a confrontation breaks out among players who are out of bounds and you must leave the spot to break it up. Don't be in a hurry to find a football. Wait for all of the players to clear the sideline before you worry about relaying a ball into the middle.

## Understand forward progress.

You will have forward progress on the vast majority of scrimmage plays. How important is that task? An entire chapter of this book has been dedicated to it. Still, here are some basic concepts.

Move downfield to the forward progress line as quickly as you can, then move toward the ball at a 90-degree angle; that's called squaring off. Don't approach the ball in an arc; that's called "the banana" and it looks terribly unprofessional. Never jump over players. Move into the field until you encounter players. Mark the spot and watch players not directly involved in the tackle.

When you mark forward progress, stand with the downfield foot forward, shoulders parallel to the sideline, facing your fellow wing official. Your foremost foot marks the exact line. When the play is on the opposite side of the field and your partner is marking progress, mirror his position.

## Get to the goalline.

There are going to be times when a runner is simply too fast. That situation aside, it's preferable to have at least one official at the goalline every time a runner crosses it. When the ball is snapped inside team B's five yardline, the wings break to the goalline at the snap and officiate back to the ball, if necessary.

## Be decisive in short-yardage situations.

Treat the line to gain as a goalline when appropriate. For example: It's fourth and three on team B's 11 yardline. At the snap, the wings should move briskly to the eight yardline. If the runner is stopped short, work back to the ball. If he moves beyond the line to gain, officiate the play as normal. If he's stopped near the line to gain, bust in to the ball as far as you can. If you're primary on the spot, ask for the football and place it on the ground at your downfield foot.

All officials must be aware when the ball becomes dead near the line to gain. Tossing the ball to the umpire and then having it returned to a wing for a measurement looks uncoordinated and creates doubt that the ball will be put back exactly where it became dead.

CHAPTER TWO

# SNAP, TACKLE, BACK

"Once you step on the ... field, you're in a vacuum. It's just like you turn off everything outside that field.

— NFL line judge Gary Arthur

**It** sounds a little bit like a slogan for a breakfast cereal, but snap, tackle, back is a lyrical reminder for wing officials. It's a basic mantra used to program the observation of keys when the ball is put into play on a scrimmage down.

Let's break it down.

## Snap

Along with the referee and umpire, you must observe action before the snap. Those duties include counting players, checking the legality of team A's formation, observing players in motion, taking note of shifts and spotting false starts and encroachment. Wings also are responsible for ensuring the play begins with a legal snap.

## Tackle

At the snap, your focus should be on the initial block of the tackle. If it's a run block, you can momentarily disregard your key receiver. If the tackle drops back to pass block, you've got the receiver.

A quick look at the initial contact, however, can help you determine how long you need to spend on observing that block.

In PlayPic A, the defensive end (right) is head-up on the offensive tackle. When the ball is snapped and the quarterback begins his drop into the pocket, the tackle immediately engages the end (PlayPic B). If the end clearly beats the tackle, you may see a shirt grab or arm hook.

In other situations, the tackle retreats and is not confronted by a defender (PlayPic C). To concentrate on a player who is not engaged with or threatening an opponent is known as "officiating air" and is to be avoided. Instead, you can concentrate totally on the receivers in your coverage area.

**When a defensive player (right) is "head-up" on the opponent, expect a one-on-one battle between the opponents.**

Blocking in front of the runner will be intense as the offensive lineman tries to keep himself between the runner and the opponent.

If a blocker is not engaged with an opponent, look elsewhere.

## Back

A glance at the nearest back will let you see if he's going to be blocking, getting the ball or flaring out of the backfield as a receiver. Depending on the formation and action of other receivers, he may demand your attention throughout the play.

That all makes sense and it sounds easy. But there's more to it. Formations, game situation, formations and player actions are variables that may force you to hone in on different players or other areas for varying lengths of time.

Let's start with the blocking. If the wide receiver blocks back toward the snap, you must see the entire block, which may or may not be legal. The block must be above the waist and in front of or to the side of the offensive player.

Even if you have a clear view of the tackle's block, you can't always stay with that block long enough to witness a follow-through or possible takedown. A significant hold will probably not take place on that initial charge by the tackle.

A tight end who blocks at the line will tend to obscure the action of the tackle. You can be screened and straightlined out of a chance to see the whole block of a "second-man-in" along the line of scrimmage.

What's more, if a defender moves to the line to challenge a split end, you are obliged to witness that encounter. You can't look off while a defender tries to manhandle that eligible receiver. At the snap, that action has to be your sole focus.

## Back Out of the Backfield

Then there's the additional dilemma of that back running laterally out of the backfield. You must adjust your gaze to pick up that back almost at once. A quarterback scooting along the line on an option play will get outside the free-blocking zone in a matter of a few seconds. The pitchman may already have preceded him. That's the first back out of the backfield. The reality is that you cannot watch a charge by the tackle.

It is so tempting to watch the snap exchange and handoff instead of shifting focus at once to wideout keys. Wing-officials-as-spectators (ball watchers) will not do intrinsic harm when working games involving teams that are run-oriented. You can watch a tight end fire out and block, and you can see the tackle initiate contact.

Complications arise, though, when teams spread flankers, slots and wideouts, and those wideouts endeavor earnestly to help a play succeed. That is, sometimes wideouts are simply decoys, designated to extend defenses. Someone has to guard them, threat or no threat. Then you usually must watch them at the snap.

But not always. If an end is split and there is no slot or flanker, a crew may agree that the back judge has responsibility for that end (particularly if he's on the strong side of the formation). In such situations you may indeed observe the tackle and stay with him on his follow-through. In most cases that simply means watching the stand-up hand-to-hand contact with a defender and anticipating a sweep. Few players actually execute genuine blocks with shoulder pads anymore.

If there's a slot inside that split end, you can keep the slot in your peripheral vision, observe the offensive tackle and shift to the slot in the backfield as a secondary key. By setting up as a back the slot will have to move at least a few steps before contacting an opponent. You can stay focused on the tackle for a second or two before seeing if the slot intends either to block someone in the defensive secondary or else motor out on a pass route. In either case, both wideouts will telegraph the play, almost at once. And you can move downfield to watch the play unfold.

But you cannot go far without looking back to see if a quarterback option play is developing, an end run moves toward you (in which case you may have to pick up pulling linemen) or if a swing pass may be in the offing.

So to be successful in all eventualities, you must shift focus rapidly in a carefully chosen sequence in order to view vital elements of various plays and player actions. It's not a simplistic, "I'll watch those two players all the time."

## Other Formations

You can treat a lone flanker or a trips setup much the same way. Tight end primary key, wideout secondary key, tackle almost an afterthought and if eligibles take off on fly patterns, leave the deep responsibilities to the back judge.

The "belly" series or option attack is another challenge entirely, presenting a host of precise requirements.

Wideouts dashing toward the spot of the snap will announce that a play is coming your way. You've got to see that contact, making sure no illegal blocks take place. If the quarterback is sprinting toward you, you must program yourself not to blow an inadvertent whistle when it looks like the handoff recipient has been stopped. The quarterback is likely to keep the ball after a ride or quick fake.

When the option quarterback reaches the edge, he'll make a decision to either pitch it or keep it and dart upfield. The jurisdiction in that case should be clear-cut: You take the ball carrier swinging wide. That means you stay with the runner but shift attention to the pitchman if the deep back gets the ball.

The referee takes the player without the ball, meaning he takes care of the quarterback who has released it. That's a big responsibility because the quarterback may be close to or beyond the line when he tosses it and the sweeping back may have chugged too far ahead of the toss, making the pitch a forward pass. Who's to judge? Only you are in a position (outside the sidelines) to make those distinctions.

At the risk of redundancy, working the wing is not just a matter of paying homage to a catchy phrase. The good news is, much of what is described here will be much easier to discern on the field. Ink on paper cannot do it justice.

# CHAPTER THREE

# FORWARD PROGRESS AND SPOTTING THE BALL

"The most important part of forward progress is squaring off your spot on the sideline before you ever start onto the field of play and then busting onto the field hard (along with the head linesman) and selling your spot with authority."

— NFL line judge Mark Steinkerchner

**Forward** progress is to a wing official what balls and strikes are to a plate umpire. Few plays don't require the head linesman or line judge (or both) to determine the spot. Officials who struggle with the concept of forward progress will catch a lot of grief from coaches and may find themselves moved to other positions.

Barring the unusual events of an inadvertent whistle or the runner's helmet coming completely off, the runner's advancement can end four ways: he is down by rule, he steps out of bounds, he fumbles the ball out of bounds or his forward movement is stopped. It is the latter that makes the subject of forward progress so intriguing. The judgment as to when and where the play ended can also determine if there was a change of possession.

The challenge officials will always face is noting two places at once: the spot where and if the runner is down by rule and the spot where the forward-most point of the ball is when that happens.

Every runner's progress is exactly the same: the forward-most part of the ball when it's declared dead in possession of the runner (when progress is declared dead inbounds or where it crossed the sideline when declared dead out of bounds), whether the ball is parallel to or perpendicular to the sideline.

In the vast majority of cases, it is obvious the ball has become dead by rule. A runner is down when any part of his body other than a hand or foot touches the ground (the ankle or wrist are considered part of the foot or hand, respectively). Additionally, a runner is not down if any part of his body touches another player (teammate or opponent) who is lying on the ground.

The spot where the runner's knee touches the ground is seldom, if ever, the forward progress spot. Because the location of the ball and the location of the knee are rarely at exactly the same place, the spot the ball is located at the moment the ball becomes dead is the forward progress spot.

PlayPic A (next page) illustrates a typical scenario. The runner's left knee is down, hence the ball is dead. The ball in his right hand is well forward of his knee. The dead-ball spot is where the ball is located, not the knee.

Once a runner's forward progress is ruled to have stopped while being tackled and the runner is then driven backward or sideways, forward progress is exactly where the ball was at the moment the backward or sideways motion occurs. The whistle is blown and the play ended. No fumble may occur behind the forward progress spot because the ball is dead by rule. If that action occurs near the sideline and the ball is not beyond the line-to-gain, signal the clock to continue running to indicate the ball became dead inbounds. Keep your head up and eyes on the players as they go out of bounds.

**PlayPic®**

**A**

The ball should be spotted at the foremost point of the ball, not where the knee hit the ground.

## Airborne Receiver or Runner

Forward progress for an airborne receiver is the spot where he gains possession and maintains control of the ball while being tackled and driven backward while still in the air. Should an airborne receiver have possession, be contacted, lose possession, then regain possession prior to hitting the ground with anything but his hand or foot, his progress is the spot where he last gained possession.

When the runner is airborne as he crosses the sideline, forward progress is where the ball crosses the plane of the sideline, not where the ball is when the runner first touches out of bounds.

## Inbounds Plays

A common situation involves the runner having the ball is in his possession being swarmed while he is still upright or "stood up" by several defensive players so that his voluntary movement appears to be stopped. In that case, the covering official should hesitate briefly to ensure the runner has indeed been stopped. If so, the whistle should be blown. The ball became dead when forward movement was stopped and not where the ball was when the whistle was blown.

Do not allow a "cheap turnover" after progress has stopped. Unless the ball became loose on the initial contact that stopped progress, the correct ruling is no fumble. If the covering official has any doubt when the ball became loose, the ruling should be that the ball was dead before the fumble.

The greatest degree of judgment is required when the runner is knocked backward and continues to drive his legs. The runner may be able to move forward while in control of an opponent or he may actually free himself of the opponent's grasp. If the runner momentarily frees himself from the tacklers, the progress spot is not automatically erased and the official should hesitate before whistling the play dead to ensure the runner's forward progress has been stopped.

## Plays at the Sideline

Many officials struggle when the idea of forward progress shifts to the sidelines. The principle is the same as it is in the middle of the field.

An associated consideration is the clock. If the runner is stopped in the field of play, the clock is not stopped, but if he went out of bounds, the clock is stopped. A runner who is contacted by an opponent and crosses the sideline as he is moving forward has been forced out of bounds and the clock is stopped. If the runner is displaced laterally or backward and goes out of bounds, his progress has been stopped in the field of play and the clock continues to run unless it is stopped for another reason such as a foul or the awarding of a new series. The wing official will indicate the clock should run by using the wind the clock signal.

In MechaniGram B, A1 runs to his left. About a foot inbounds at team A's 38 yardline, A1's forward progress is stopped (A) but he stays on his feet. A1 is shoved or falls backward and goes out of bounds at team A's 36 yardline (B). The ball should be spotted at the hashmark on team A's 38 yardline because that's as far as A1 advanced. Assuming that neither a first down nor a change of possession is involved, because the runner's forward progress was stopped inbounds, the game clock should continue to run

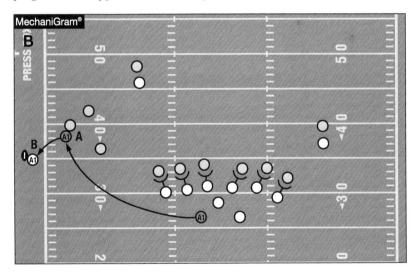

**Progress is to the 39 yardline.**

even if A1 subsequently goes out of bounds.

MechaniGram C illustrates A1 being tackled from behind. A1's advance ended because he went out of bounds, and the ball is spotted where it crossed the sideline when the ball became dead by rule. Because A1's progress ended out of bounds, the game clock should be stopped.

The last possible scenario is seen in MechaniGram D. A1 is driven out of bounds sideways. Again, A1 is given the benefit of his farthest advance. His progress was stopped inbounds and the clock should continue to run.

When a runner steps on the sideline, wing officials almost always mark the progress spot where the runner's foot contacted the sideline. That usually is a fairly accurate spot. However, since the progress spot is at the location of the ball, the spot where the runner's foot touched the sideline is

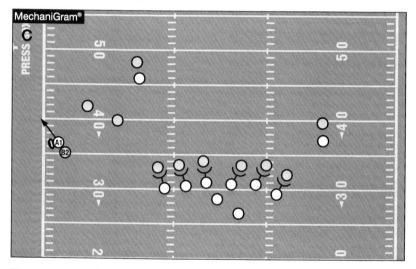

**The progress spot is where the ball crossed the sideline.**

not necessarily the correct location.

Good wing officials can accurately discern the spot based on the ball location. If the runner steps out of bounds with his lead foot and is carrying the ball in his outside arm, the location of the ball and the spot where his foot touches the sideline are virtually identical. However, if the ball is in his inside arm, it should be spotted about the length of the ball behind the spot where his foot touched out of bounds. The extra precision is most appropriate for plays that end near the goalline or the line-to-gain.

If the runner is approaching the line-to-gain, he may extend the ball to increase the point of advancement. If that occurs, the dead-ball spot is where the ball was when the runner stepped out of bounds.

## Behind the Neutral Zone

When the wings read pass, they will be downfield on pass coverage.

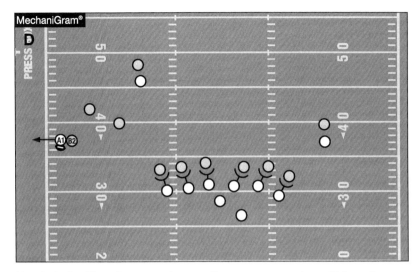

**The clock should continue to run because the progress was stopped inbounds.**

Thus the referee will almost always be responsible for progress spots on quarterback sacks.

Other runs that end behind the neutral zone are the responsibility of the wings just as any other running play.

## Plays at the Pylon

The goalline pylons are placed at the intersection of the goallines extended and the sideline. They not only assist in making out-of-bounds calls, they can help an official determine whether a touchback has occurred and, most importantly, whether a touchdown has been scored. Because the goalline pylons are placed on the sideline, they are entirely out of bounds. The end zone is entirely inbounds. For practical purposes, the pylons are considered out of bounds in the end zone.

Whenever a runner is contacted near a goalline pylon, it requires the coordination of both the back judge and a wing official to get the play right. For a runner who is still touching the ground inbounds, the goalline plane is extended out of bounds. If the ball is held outside the sideline plane and breaks the goalline plane extended, it is a touchdown.

The wing official is responsible for determining if the runner stayed inbounds, while the back judge (when in position at the goalline) must rule if the ball broke the plane of the goalline. Those officials must communicate with each other before either makes a call. After making eye contact, a simple bob of the head indicates the runner was inbounds and the ball broke the plane.

A ball in player possession is out of bounds when the runner or the ball touches anything, other than another player or official, which is on or outside the sideline or end line.

**The airborne runner's forward progress is where the ball crosses the sideline.**

In PlayPic E, the runner dives for the goalline but comes up short. In that case, the spot where the ball becomes dead is under the foremost point of the ball in possession of the runner when he crosses the plane of the sideline — in this case, at team B's one yardline. No touchdown is scored since the runner was airborne and was not touching inbounds when the ball broke the plane of the goalline extended.

Remember that a ball that contacts the pylon is considered to be in the end zone. If it is in possession of a runner when it touches the pylon, it is a touchdown, touchback or safety. If the ball is loose when it touches the pylon, it is a touchback or a safety.

## Covering the Play

The manner in which the offensive line blocks will most often tell you what type of play is being run. When the offensive linemen fire out, it's usually a run. When they drop back to form the pocket, think pass. When linemen pull, it's likely a pass to the flat (the area in the offensive backfield outside the normal position of the tackle) or a sweep.

On runs between the tackles and to the opposite side, use the side shuffle mechanic to stay even with the play. Shuffling your feet and moving laterally keeps your shoulders square to the play and puts you in position to get an accurate spot. When the runner is downed move toward the pile while indicating the next down. If the line-to-gain has been reached, stop the clock and inform the referee verbally or by using the crew

**PlayPic® F**

This signal is used to tell the referee a first down has been achieved.

communication signal (PlayPic F).

If the runner bursts through the defense and takes off on a sprint, turn parallel to the sideline and accelerate to follow the play. Trail the runner while outside the sideline. Remember that in addition to the runner, you must watch action in the area around the runner. That's where illegal blocks and other fouls occur.

## Cross-Field Spotting

Long-distance calls are to be avoided whenever possible, particularly when it involves another official's area of coverage. If you're going to fish in someone else's pond, you'd better catch a whale, not a minnow. One exception is cross-field spotting. When a play occurs at a sideline, the covering wing official often has to keep some distance for safety sake and it's difficult to get an accurate spot. In that case, the opposite wing must step up.

In MechaniGram G, the quarterback takes a one- or two-step drop and fires to the wideout who is a few yards beyond the line and on the line judge's side. If team B is using press coverage, the receiver will be contacted

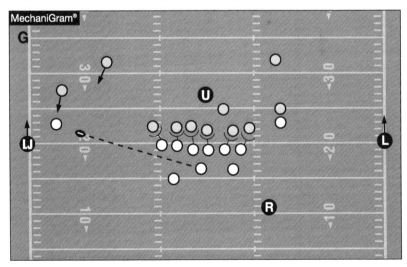

**MechaniGram® G**

The wings flow downfield for pass coverage.

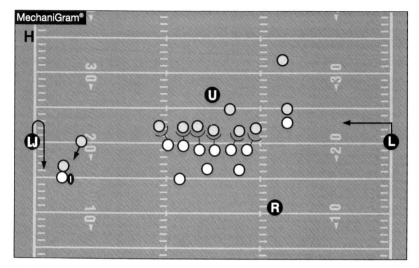

The linesman holds the spot while the line judge attends to players.

shortly after the pass arrives. The defender will often drive the receiver back behind the line, sometimes several yards. The line judge must flow back with those players, watching for fouls and determining if the runner stepped out of bounds. From across the field, the linesman hustles to the spot and marks the progress (MechaniGram H). Knowing that he's been driven off the spot, the line judge can look up, see the linesman's spot and casually go to it.

Cross-field spotting is an important part of the job. The wings must have confidence in each other, knowing that the other official will help out when needed. If for whatever reason (say, a scuffle has broken out) the opposite wing is unable to provide a spot, the covering official must give his best estimate.

## Sliding Runner

Forward progress is determined by the forward point of the ball when it becomes dead. The ball may become dead because the runner is down or because the runner goes out of bounds. A runner who slides across the sideline will want the extra yards gained from the slide, but they don't count.

In PlayPic I, the runner's left side hits the ground inbounds. The runner then gains yardage and slides several yards beyond the sideline. Not only should the ball be placed where it was when the runner's hip, elbow and knee contacted the ground, but unless a first down was gained, the clock should continue to run.

There is no high school rule similar to the NCAA and NFL rules which specifically cover a quarterback who scrambles beyond the line and slides to

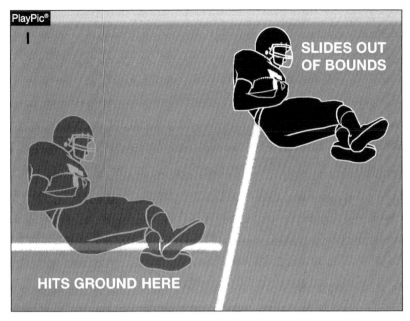

PlayPic®

I

SLIDES OUT OF BOUNDS

HITS GROUND HERE

**The ball is spotted at the yardline it was over when the runner's hip or knee touched the ground, not where the slide out of bounds ended.**

"give himself up." A runner who slides is protected from contact, whether he slides head first or feet first. Officials should practice good dead-ball officiating in those cases. It is ripe for a defender to pin down the runner with an elbow or forearm.

It is not uncommon for a player who hits the ground in the manner seen in the PlayPic to lose possession of the ball. Remember that the ball is dead when the runner is down and, in the case illustrated, the ground cannot cause a fumble.

## Basic Mechanics

Progress should be indicated by using the downfield foot. Keep your head up and observe players while marking a spot. Do not go around or jump over players to mark progress. Move into the field until you approach players, then stop. From that position you will be able to observe all the play around the pile while marking the progress spot.

When possible, the spotting official should place the ball at his foot on all plays that end outside the numbers toward the sidelines. When possible, leave the ball on the ground and retrieve a new ball for the umpire to spot the new ball at the hashmark.

If a spot is close to a first down, the spotting official must come all the way to the spot where the play ended indicating to the umpire that "It's close," or "Let's take a look." Wait for players to clear your path and then continue to spot the ball. The umpire shall hand (not toss) the ball to an official that has crashed into the field for a critical spot. umpires appreciate a wing official that verbalizes confidence in their spot. That avoids confusion when the umpire looks for a wing official with the best spot.

The line judge has primary responsibility for determining if a first down has been achieved since he can see the lead stake on the chains from across the field. If the ball is clearly beyond the stake, he will stop the clock and signal the first down to the referee using the crew communication signal described above. If the ball is clearly short, he will announce the number of the next down. If it is questionable, he will stop the clock and signal for the referee to come forward and look at it. He may recommend a measurement to the referee.

Measurement mechanics are covered elsewhere in this book.

## Squaring Off

Squaring off, as opposed to moving toward the spot in arcs, lends credibility to the call. It also helps the opposite wing mirror the spot. MechaniGram J illustrates a running play covered by the line judge.

Note that the line judge remains out of bounds and moves downfield until reaching the dead-ball spot. He then squares at a 90-degree angle and uses his downfield foot to indicate the spot.

"The most important part of forward progress," said veteran NFL line judge Mark Steinkerchner, "is squaring off your spot on the sideline before you ever start onto the field of play and then busting onto the field hard (along with the head linesman) and selling your spot with authority. 'With authority' is the key because if you hesitate too much or come onto the field at half speed or waver off of your line onto the field no one will believe you, even if you are right."

Officials should keep their heads on a swivel, making a visual sweep of the other players to watch for dead-ball fouls. Casting your eyes toward the ground could cause you to miss a foul that might lead to more trouble. Avoid leaving the progress spot until the spot has been picked up by the umpire or referee and they have indicated that to you.

Do not go around or jump over players to mark progress. Move into the field until you approach players, then stop. If a spot is close to the line-to-gain, the covering official must come all the way to the spot where the play ended. The primary official responsible for determining the forward progress spot is the wing official who can actually see the ball when the play is declared dead, not based on what side of the field the play ends.

"(The wings) must mirror each other on every play," said Steinkerchner. "One thing that works well is pinching in hard if something unusual happens. For instance, if the runner is down just before the ball comes loose or the runner's knee is down and he tries to extend the ball for a first down, pinching in hard tells the other wing man you have the correct spot."

When possible, the spotting official should place the ball at his foot on all plays that end between the numbers and the sideline. When possible, leave the ball on the ground and retrieve a new ball for the umpire to spot the new ball at the hashmark.

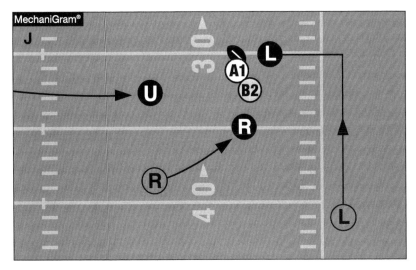

**Squaring off at a 90-degree angle looks professional and improves accuracy.**

## Progress at the Goalline

Forward progress at the goalline is often more difficult because team A may use a tight formation with no gaps between linemen. In response, team B will use a tight line with the majority of its players on or just off the line of scrimmage.

Move perpendicularly in from the sideline to the spot. Don't veer around players and don't cut through the end zone if the ball hasn't crossed the goalline because those bring your navigation into question. If you know exactly where the spot is, go to it and place your foot on it. If you have "estimated" forward progress, get the ball from the umpire to mark the spot, place it down with authority and sell the call so that it appears you know the exact spot.

"As players start to complain," advises Steinkerchner, "you must confidently tell them, 'That is the spot.' You don't want to say you saw the ball at that spot because they will know you couldn't."

Officials do have the benefit of knowing the players created a pile and were otherwise occupied during the play.

"Remember, they have no idea where the spot was either, but if you sound unsure or say, 'That's where I think the ball was,' you've lost credibility for that call and the rest of your calls,.'" Steinkerchner said.

## Caseplays

Test your understanding of forward progress and spotting with these caseplays:

**Play 1:** First and 10 on team A's 20 yardline. A2 takes a handoff and (a) is sent flying by a shoestring tackle, dives forward and his right shoulder is first to touch the ground at team A's 27 yardline; (b) is grabbed by the knees, which touch the ground at team A's 25 yardline while the rest of his body is nearly upright as he thrusts the ball forward and it contacts the ground at team A's 26 yardline; or (c) is stopped upright at team A's 23 yardline by B2 and B3. Ruling 1: In (a), the ball is spotted where it was (slightly behind team A's 27 yardline) when A2's shoulder touched the ground. In (b), the dead-ball spot is team A's 25 yardline, where the ball was when A2's knees touched the ground. The thrust to team A's 26 yardline was with a dead ball. In (c), although A2 was never "downed," his forward progress was stopped at team A's 23 yardline.

**Play 2:** Runner A4 plunges into the pack at his 35 yardline and is contacted by several team B players. A4 is (a) carried back several yards and dumped at his 31 yardline, or (b) pushed backed to his 32 yardline where he breaks free and continues to run before he is tackled at his 33 yardline. Ruling 2: In (a), A4's voluntary movement was stopped at his 35 yardline, the dead-ball spot. In (b), since A4 was able to break free and continue voluntary movement, his forward progress is where the ball was when he contacted the ground. In that case, that is team A's 33 yardline.

**Play 3:** Third and 15 on team A's 35 yardline. A1 drops back to pass to his 28 yardline; he (a) decides to run and just as he takes a step forward to his 29 yardline, or (b) while he is stationary, is contacted by B6 who firmly grasps him and without being unnecessarily rough, swings him around. A1 comes to the ground at his 25 yardline. Ruling 3: In either case, A1 is given forward progress at the spot he was contacted by B6. In (a), the dead-ball spot is team A's 29 yardline and in (b), team A's 28 yardline.

# CHAPTER FOUR

# PREGAME AND COIN TOSS

Just like the players, officials need to stretch and warm up before a game. Run down to the pylons and then run to check the other end zone. It's a great way to warm up and will show you're ready to go. Calisthenics or stretching should be performed out of bounds near the end zone.

**According** to the rules, the officials' authority begins 30 minutes prior to the scheduled game time — an earlier time if required by the state association — or as soon thereafter as they are able to be present. There is plenty to do in the time between the officials' arrival and the start of the game. Here is a rundown.

## Preliminaries

All officials should inspect the field. If potholes, broken glass or other hazards are discovered, ask game management to have the problem taken care of immediately. If the field is marked for another sport (many football fields are also used for soccer), make sure the crew knows which lines are being used for football. Make sure the goalposts are straight and free of decoration and that the goalpost pads are securely fastened. Check the pylons to ensure they are properly placed.

Spend some time warming up. Run from point to point as you do your pregame checks. Run down to the pylons and then run to check the other end zone. It's a great way to warm up and will show you're ready to go. Calisthenics or stretching should be performed out of bounds near the end zone

Casually observe both teams for information that will be helpful during the game. Watch both teams without giving the appearance they are being inspected. Pay attention to player actions similar to those you will see during the game. Players play the way they practice. Things to look for include: How strong are the punters' and kickers' legs? How is the wind affecting kicks? How does the kicked ball spin? How does the team line up? Do they rush the snap after getting set?

What blocking techniques are used? Do the linemen block low? Is the tight end and/or slot back in the free-blocking zone? Is the offensive line split or unbalanced? Do they use a double wide, a slot or trips? What patterns do the receivers run? On defense, do linebackers line up tight enough to be in the free blocking zone at the snap? How does the defensive line pass rush?

Avoid using pregame time for nonessential chat with players, coaches, spectators or others, especially if it could give the appearance of favoritism.

## Pregame Duties

The referee and one other official are required to meet with the head coaches before the game. Although it's traditionally the umpire who joins the referee, it is only required that one other official — possibly the linesman or line judge — participate in the meeting

The meeting with each of the head coaches may occur on or off the field, based on local practice. It is best to meet with the home coach first as he may have information about pregame ceremonies that must be relayed to the visiting coach.

The meeting should begin with the referee and crewmate introducing themselves and giving the coach a card listing names of crew members.

Ask the coach if all players are properly equipped and if there are players with guards, casts, braces, etc. that need to be inspected. Ask for the name of the "get-back coach" and give a brief discussion of sideline control and expectations.

Get the captains' numbers. Some crews also obtain the captains' names. If an official wishes to speak to a captain during the game, perhaps to seek his help in calming an angry teammate, the captain will respond better if he is called by name rather than number. Also, ask if the quarterback is right-handed or left-handed and if the place kicker and punter are right-footed or left-footed.

The referee should ask to see the footballs that are to be used and, along with the umpire and back judge, inspect and approve them so the back judge recognizes legal balls when placed under the upright. Ask if the team plans on using any unique formations or trick plays. Foreknowledge helps the crew be prepared for such instances and increases the chances the play will be officiated correctly. Avoid conversations about "what the other team does."

Remind the coach that he (not an assistant coach) may leave the team box to call a timeout as long as he remains off the playing field. That may be necessary when the ball is snapped near the goalline.

Ask if medical staff is present. If possible, meet with the athletic trainer and make introductions and ask where he or she will be located during the contest.

Ask if any special ceremony is planned. Also, if there is a planned extended halftime, make sure the coach is aware of it.

## When Duties Are Completed

The crew should meet to share the information gleaned while the teams were warming up. Avoid a midfield gathering that may interfere with pregame ceremonies and focus undue attention to the officials.

One official on each side of the field stands at the team A and team B 40 yardline and the referee rotates among all officials. Officials can swap 40 yardline locations on their side of the field. Even if discussions are productive, it may give the impression that the officials are goofing off. Discussions can wait until teams go back into the locker room or they end their pregame warmups.

Discuss unusual plays or formations either team may have either that were observed or mentioned by the coaches.

## Coin Toss

The coin toss is the first visible and formal chance to make everyone comfortable that the game will be fairly administered. It is essential that all games start with a consistent ceremony. Some aspects can be personalized without harm, but other changes can cause problems. If the referee conveys through his mannerisms that he doesn't know what he is doing, the next two-three hours will be rough going. Once a coach gets the idea the crew is not competent, everything the officials do will be suspect. At a minimum, the crew will be perceived to have a renegade approach to officiating.

Local or conference policy dictates when and where the toss takes place. The ceremony (see MechaniGram) begins with the umpire escorting to midfield the team captains (maximum of four) from the team on the side of the field that has the chains. The referee escorts the opposing captains. The line judge remains at the hashmarks on the side of the field opposite the chains and the back judge positions himself at the hashes on the opposite side during the toss. Observe players not involved in the coin toss. If each team is using its own game balls, the back judge and line judge should each have an approved game ball from the team on their sideline.

The coin toss is a good opportunity for the linesman to conduct the pregame meeting with the chain crew (See chapter 7).

When the toss is completed, the other officials join the referee and umpire in the center of the field and record the results of the toss. All officials simultaneously move to their kickoff positions.

## Second Half

Second-half choices are obtained from the head coaches. It is recommended the referee get the information in the presence of the appropriate wing official. It is best to utilize the scoreboard as reference when referring to the direction choice. On rare occasions, the referee may bring the captains together at midfield to deal with issues and problems from the first half; however, it is preferable to discuss those issues directly with the head coach.

## Overtime Procedure

If overtime is necessary, the coin toss is repeated with the visiting team again declaring heads or tails. The winner may choose defense, offense or the goal to be used. When the selections are completed, the captains of the team on offense are asked to face the goalline in the direction their team will advance and the opposing captains stand with their backs to that goalline. The referee then points to the shoulder of the captain of the team that won the toss and gives the first down signal in the appropriate direction.

For a second overtime period, the coin will not be tossed again. The loser of the overtime coin toss is given the first choice of options. If additional overtime periods are necessary, the first choice of options is alternated without a coin toss.

# CHAPTER FIVE
# KEYS

One of the arts of solid officiating is knowing when to leave your key to help out elsewhere. Sense how the play is developing and switch your focus to the action in your coverage area.

**Football** officials have a kind of telepathy to help them determine what's going to happen before it occurs. These hints are called keys.

There are two basic types of keys: "situational" and "positional" keys.

## Situational Keys

Situational keys are partially based on the down, distance, score, time remaining, offensive and defensive formations and actions of players at the snap. For example, it's third down and 11. Team A trails by two points with 1:37 to play in the fourth quarter and has the ball on its own 44 yardline. Going without a huddle, team A lines up in a shotgun formation with three receivers on the right side of the formation. All of that adds up to a pass. That hunch is confirmed when, at the snap, the offensive linemen drop back to pass block, the quarterback retreats into the pocket and the receivers run pass patterns rather than block team B's linebackers and defensive backs.

In addition to down, distance and other game factors, offensive and defensive formations provide hints as to what type of play an official can expect in a given situation. Most teams using the wishbone formation, for instance, are predominantly running teams. Teams using four-receiver sets and shotgun formations pass more times than not.

Linemen provide situational keys. Pulling linemen indicate a sweep or trap block. Retreating linemen indicate a pass. Charging linemen indicate a running play. When offensive linemen provide only passive resistance, allowing defensive linemen to penetrate the neutral zone, a screen pass often follows.

## Positional Keys

Positional keys are predetermined by the position you are working in the game. Positional keys deal more with the back judge and wing officials. The back judge's main positional key is the widest eligible receiver on the strong side of the formation (that will usually be the split end or the flanker). At the snap, the back judge first observes the tackle to see if he's run-blocking or pass-blocking, then observes the actions of his key receiver. If that player moves into another official's coverage area, the back judge shifts his attention to players who have entered his coverage area.

In order to determine positional keys, the officials must recognize the strength of the formation (strong side vs. weak side). The strong side is the side on which there are more eligible receivers outside of the tackle.

When determining keys, it doesn't matter if a player is on or off the line of scrimmage. The widest receiver is the back judge's key whether the player is a flanker (a back usually positioned wider than the tight end) or a wide out (split outside the tackle). If players are stacked, the player nearest the line of scrimmage is considered to be the widest. For example, if a flanker is stacked directly behind the tight end, the tight end is considered the widest and is the back judge's key.

A balanced formation is one in which there are the same number of eligible receivers outside the tackles on both sides of the formation. An unbalanced formation is when one side has more eligible receivers on one side than the other.

The back judge has priority in determining keys, followed by the wing men. Wing officials should not key the same player as the back judge.

The positional keys:

• Unbalanced formation — The back judge keys on the widest receiver on the strong side. The wing official on the strong side keys on the inside player of the formation, normally a flanker or wing back. The wing official on the weak side keys the end nearest his side, normally a wideout.

• Balanced formation — In a balanced formation, strength is always considered to be on the line judge's side. The back judge keys on the widest receiver (usually a split end). The wing officials key on receivers other than the back judge's key and any backs who move toward them at the snap.

• Three-receiver (trips) formation — The back judge keys on the two widest receivers and the strong side wing official keys on the inside receiver. The weak side wing official keys on the end nearest him.

• Double wing formation — Strength is declared to the line judge's side. The back judge keys the widest receiver on the line judge's side. The line judge keys the inside receiver. The linesman has both receivers on his side.

• Wishbone — Another balanced formation, which means strength is declared to line judge's side. The back judge has the end on the line judge's side. The line judge keys the backs. The linesman keys the end on his side.

## Motion

An offensive player in motion can affect positional keys. It is crucial that the back judge and wing officials know where the motion man is at the snap because the strength of the formation (and therefore the keys) may change. Legality of motion is always the responsibility of the official away from whom the player is moving.

Say team A lines up strong to the linesman's side, but the flanker on the linesman's side goes in motion toward the line judge. If the motion man gets to the line judge's side of the ball at the snap, the strength of the formation is now on the line judge's side and the keys change. The back judge now has the wideout on the line judge's side, the line judge has the motion man and the linesman has the end on his side of the line. Although the line judge is keying on the motion man's action after the snap, the linesman is responsible for watching to ensure the motion man does not cut upfield before the snap. If the motion man does not get to the opposite side of the formation before the snap, the keys do not change because the strength of the formation has not changed.

If motion turns a formation into trips, the keys for trips are in force: The back judge keys on the two widest receivers and the strong side wing official keys on the inside receiver.

# BALANCED FORMATION, STRENGTH DECLARED TO LINE JUDGE'S SIDE

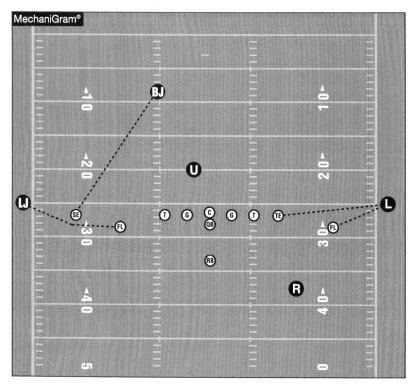

In a balanced formation, strength is always considered to be on the line judge's side. The back judge keys on the widest receiver (in this case, the split end). The line judge keys on the flanker while the linesman has both the split end and flanker on his side. Either wing official may also have the back if he runs a pass route.

# DOUBLE TIGHT ENDS, STRENGTH TO LINESMAN'S SIDE

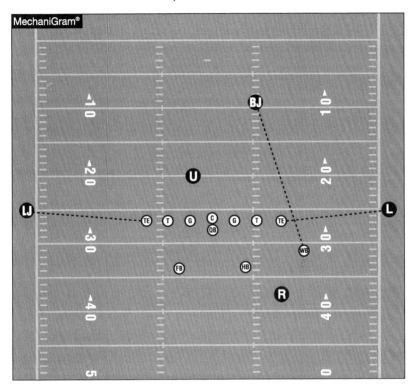

This is primarily a running formation used on short yardage, but teams sometimes throw quick passes out of this formation. The back judge keys on the widest receiver on the strong side (the wingback on the linesman's side in this case). The linesman keys on the tight end. The line judge keys on the tight end on his side. Either wing official may also have a back who runs a pass route.

# DOUBLE WING, DOUBLE TIGHT END FORMATION

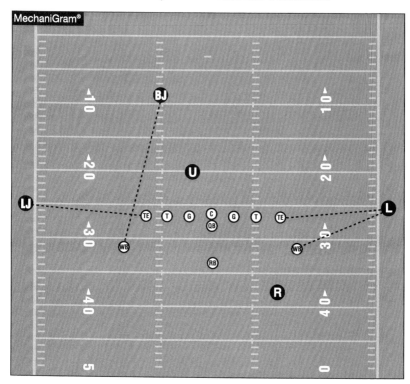

Strength is declared to the line judge's side. The back judge keys on the widest receiver on his side. In this case, that's the wingback on the line judge's side. The line judge keys on the tight end on his side. The linesman has the tight end and wingback on his side. Either wing official may also have the back if he runs a pass route.

# MOTION CHANGES STRENGTH

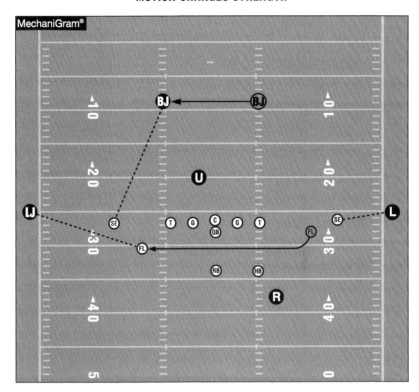

Strength was to the linesman's side, but motion changed the strength to the line judge's side. The back judge shifts position and keys on the strong side split end. The line judge keys on the flanker and the linesman keys on the split end on his side. Although the line judge is keying on the motion man's action after the snap, the linesman is responsible for watching to ensure the motion man does not cut upfield before the snap. Legality of motion is always the responsibility of the official away from whom the player is moving.

# MOTION CHANGES FORMATION FROM UNBALANCED TO BALANCED

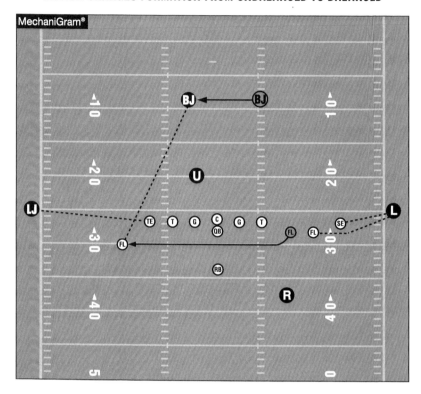

Strength was to the linesman's side, but motion changed the formation from unbalanced to balanced. In a balanced formation, strength is declared to the line judge's side. The back judge shifts position and keys on the strong side flanker. The line judge keys on the tight end and the linesman keys on the split end and flanker on his side. Although the line judge is keying on the motion man's action after the snap, the linesman is responsible for watching to ensure the motion man does not cut upfield before the snap. Legality of motion is always the responsibility of the official away from whom the player is moving.

# MOTION INTO TRIPS

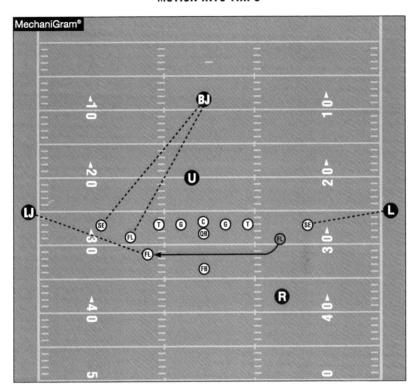

Motion by the flanker turned a balanced formation into a trips formation to the line judge's side. The back judge keys the two widest receivers. In this case, it's the set flanker and the split end on the line judge's side. The line judge keys on the motion man and the linesman keys the end on his side of the line. Although the line judge is keying on the motion man's action after the snap, the linesman is responsible for watching to ensure the motion man does not cut upfield before the snap. Legality of motion is always the responsibility of the official away from whom the player is moving.

# MOTION DOESN'T CHANGE STRENGTH

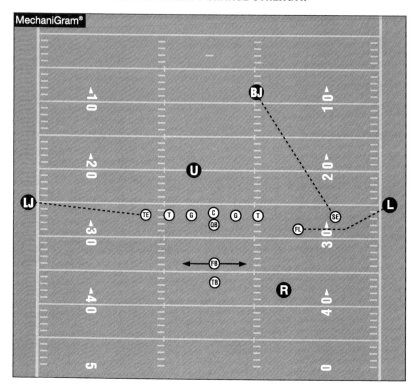

Strength is to the linesman's side. Even if the back goes in motion to the line judge's side, strength is not considered to have changed. The back judge keys the split end and the linesman keys on the flanker. The line judge keys on the split end. Either wing official may also have the back if he runs a pass route.

# STRAIGHT T

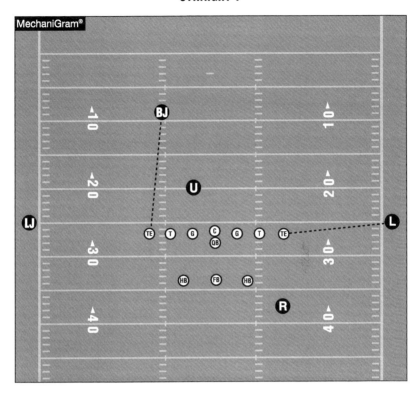

This is primarily a running formation, but on passing downs teams sometimes move a tight end to split end. It's a balanced formation, so strength is declared to the line judge's side. The back judge keys on the tight end on the line judge's side. The linesman keys on the weak side tight end. The line judge has no formal key, but should look through the tight end to observe the tackle on his side and observe the halfback after the snap. Either wing official may have a back who runs a pass route.

# STRENGTH TO LINESMAN'S SIDE, WEAK SIDE SPLIT END

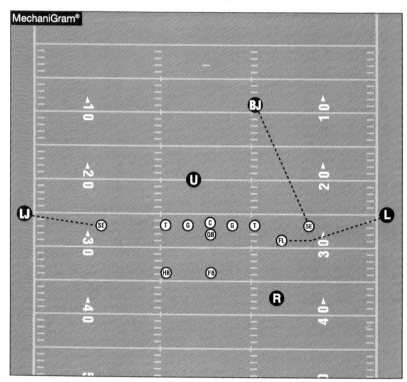

The back judge keys on the strong side split end and the linesman keys on the flanker. The line judge keys the split end on his side. The fullback will likely stay in the backfield for pass protection, but the halfback may run a pass route. If the route is to the line judge's side, the line judge takes him.

# STRENGTH TO LINESMAN'S SIDE, WEAK SIDE TIGHT END

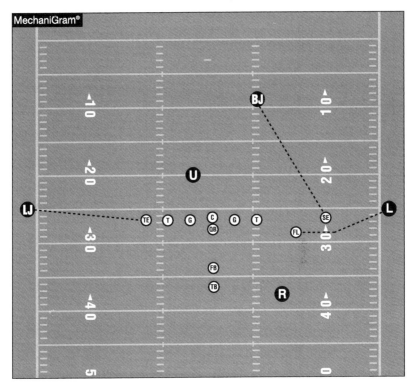

The back judge keys on the split end and the linesman keys on the flanker. The line judge keys the tight end. The fullback will likely stay in the backfield for pass protection, but the tailback may run a pass route. If the route is to the line judge's side, the line judge takes him.

# TRIPS TO LINESMAN'S SIDE

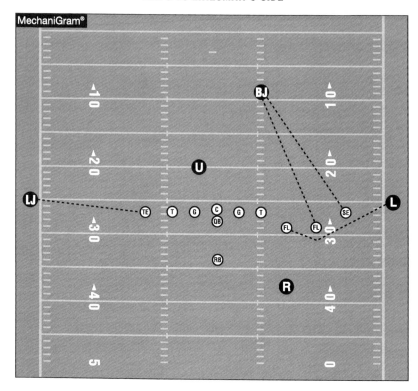

The back judge keys on the two widest receivers and the strong side wing official keys on the inside receiver. The line judge keys on the end nearest him. Either wing official may also have the back if he runs a pass route.

# UNBALANCED FORMATION, STRENGTH TO LINE JUDGE'S SIDE

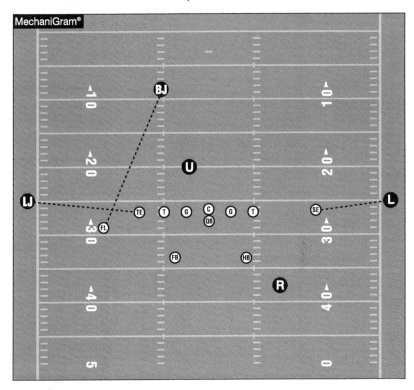

The back judge keys on the flanker and the line judge keys on the tight end. The linesman keys on the split end on his side. Either wing official may also have a back running a pass route.

# VEER

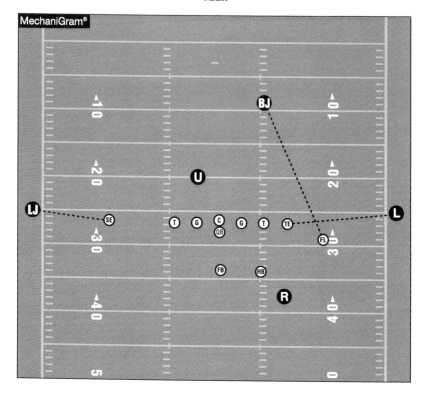

Although primarily a running formation, teams will occasionally throw to the flanker or split end. In this example, strength is to the linesman's side. The back judge keys the flanker and the linesman keys the tight end. The line judge keys on the split end on his side. The fullback's primary function is as a blocker.

# WISHBONE

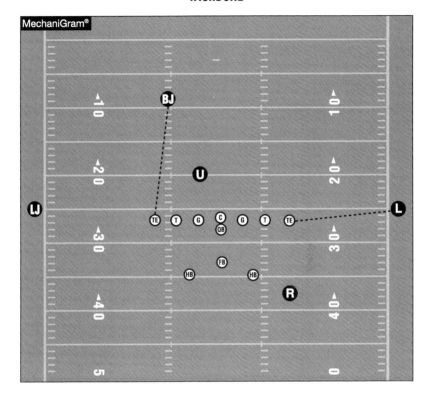

A balanced formation, which means strength is declared to line judge's side. The back judge keys the tight end on the line judge's side. The line judge keys the backs. The linesman keys the tight end on his side.

# REFEREE AND UMPIRE KEYS

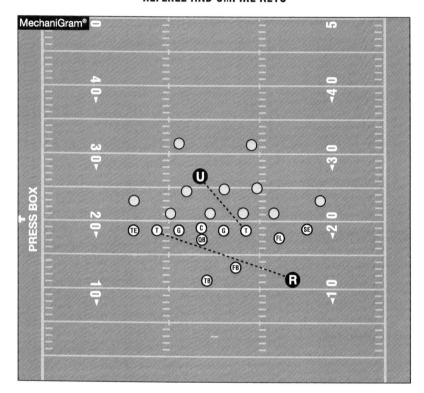

Regardless of the formation, the referee and umpire key on the opposite-side tackle. In all but the rarest cases, that means the referee keys on the left tackle and the umpire on the right tackle.

# CHAPTER SIX

# POSITIONING AND COVERAGE

"There are a lot of small things that we do during the game mechanically and ruleswise to prepare us for the next down and the next series."

— NFL line judge Mark Perlman

# FREE KICK COVERAGE ZONES

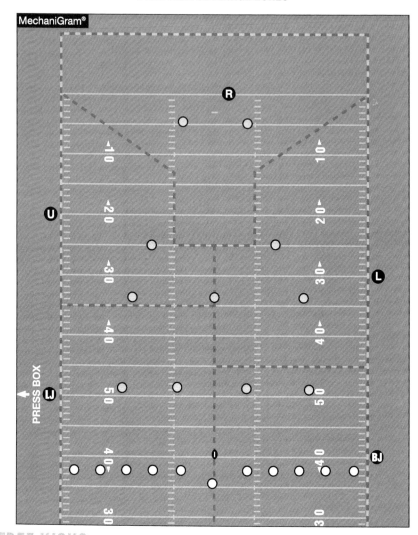

# Free Kicks

If the ball blows off the tee just prior to the kick, the back judge should sound his whistle and the ball should be re-teed.

If the kick is down the middle of the field, the referee stays with the runner to about team R's 25 yardline. If the return is to the umpire's side and as wide as the hashmark, the umpire picks up coverage and stays with the runner to team R's 35 yardline, where the line judge takes over. If the kick is to the opposite side and as wide as the hashmark, the linesman takes up the coverage and stays with the runner to about team R's 35 yardline, where he gives up coverage to the back judge.

If the umpire is responsible for the initial coverage of the runner, the referee cleans up behind the play, but must move cautiously in case team R runs a reverse or the runner reverses his field.

After the ball is kicked, the linesman moves quickly downfield while the line judge drifts downfield, maintaining coverage of the sideline. After the kick, the back judge moves toward the center of the field no more than 10-15 yards while maintaining inside-out coverage. The back judge is responsible for team K's goalline.

On kicks inside team R's five yardline, the referee is responsible for determining whether the momentum exception applies and whether the kick is to be ruled a touchback. If a touchback occurs, the referee should move quickly toward the middle of the field to prevent late hits on receivers.

## Free Kicks After a Safety

The coverage areas and mechanics are the same for the free kick that follows a safety.

The back judge should be at team K's 20 yardline, the umpire and linesman at team K's 30 yardline and the position of the remaining officials is adjusted accordingly.

## Field Goal Attempt by Free Kick After a Fair Catch

If team K attempts a field goal by free kick after a fair catch (or awarded fair catch), the referee and line judge move behind the upright. The line judge rules whether or not the kick cleared the crossbar while the referee determines if the kick was between the uprights.

The remaining officials assume their normal positions for a free kick.

## Scrimmage Plays

On a running play, the referee focuses on the ball, the runner and the blocking around the runner. If the play goes to the opposite side, the referee should move toward or parallel to the line of the scrimmage and maintain a position approximately in line with the runner. Overaggressiveness is to be avoided in case the play is a reverse. If the play is to the referee's side, the referee moves behind the play and is responsible for the runner until he crosses the neutral zone or turns upfield. The referee should watch the handoff or the pitchout, see the runner head outside the free-blocking zone, and watch to see that no one contacts the quarterback before drifting along to follow the play. He will not have much to observe besides the quarterback because little significant action is likely to take place behind the runner, and the runner himself is being watched by the appropriate wing official.

On passing plays, the referee observes blocking by his keys and is alert for defenders who threaten the quarterback. The referee should be wide and deep enough so he does not have to move if the quarterback drops back into the pocket. If the quarterback rolls to either direction, the referee must move with him, keeping at least a 10-yard buffer.

If the quarterback scrambles away from the referee, the referee needs to keep pace. If the quarterback scrambles toward the referee, the referee needs to move to the sideline, keeping his buffer as long as possible. The referee is responsible for the spot if the runner goes out of bounds behind the line of scrimmage on either sideline. If the runner goes out of bounds into the bench area, the referee follows the play into the bench area and help escort players out of the bench area.

The referee's main focus is the passer and must stay with him until he is not threatened. Once the pass has been released, the referee shouts "Gone!" to help prevent roughing the passer but continues to observe the passer. By maintaining spacing between himself and the quarterback, the referee will widen his field of vision.

If the flight of the pass is altered because the passer's arm is hit by a defender, the referee must determine whether the resultant loose ball is a forward pass or a fumble. If the referee rules the play to be an incomplete pass, he must blow his whistle and signal emphatically. If the play results in a fumble, the referee may beanbag the spot where possession was lost and continue officiating. Bagging the spot is optional because a fumble behind the line is a loose-ball play and the basic spot for penalty enforcement will be the previous spot.

Only the referee flags intentional grounding, but because he won't see where the ball landed, he'll need help from another official. Other members of the crew should immediately volunteer information regarding whether or not the ball was thrown into an area occupied by an eligible offensive receiver. If an eligible receiver was nearby, the flag can be picked up. If the referee does not throw his flag and is told the ball went into an area not occupied by an eligible offensive receiver, it is acceptable to throw a late flag, which should be "soft tossed" to the spot of the pass.

Similarly, illegal forward passes are the primary responsibility of the referee, aided by the umpire. As he trails the quarterback, the referee should move to the spot of the pass to judge whether it was thrown from beyond the line of scrimmage. If it is clearly a foul, he should drop his flag at the spot of the pass. If the spot is questionable, he should drop his beanbag. In either case, he must continue to officiate.

If the quarterback is sacked, the referee determines the progress spot and observes players as they unpile. Avoid using a beanbag to mark the spot; hustle to it while officiating the dead-ball activity.

Until the referee blows the ready for play signal, the umpire should stand with his feet straddling the ball. After the signal, the umpire moves to his position.

Umpires must determine the point of attack because of the potential for holding, chop blocks and other fouls.

Plays that end in a side zone may require the umpire to move outside the hashmark and toward the sideline in order to clean up behind the play. When play swings around to one side, the umpire should turn his attention to the blocking ahead of the runner and should prepare to cross outside the hashmark if the runner is downed in the side zone near the sideline. The umpire can help get the ball back to the hashmark and set it at the progress spot.

On pass plays, the umpire must step up and reach the line of scrimmage. That takes the umpire out of short pass routes and puts him in a position to judge ineligibles downfield and passes thrown from beyond the line of scrimmage.

When the pass is thrown, the umpire pivots to follow the flight of the ball. The umpire has catch/trap responsibility if the receiver is facing the umpire.

Before the snap, the wing officials identify the eligible receivers on their side of the field and count to ensure team A has at least seven players on the line of scrimmage. If the receiver nearest the official is in the offensive backfield, the wing uses the extended arm signal to alert the opposite wing. Legality of motion is always the responsibility of the official away from whom the player is moving, even if the player reverses his motion.

Because they will mark forward progress the vast majority of the time, the line judge and linesman must be especially alert for quick-hitting running plays into the line. On runs to the opposite side of the field, the off wing must clean up after the play.

The wings have to follow receivers downfield but should look back to see if a passer is truly setting up to pass. On quick passes in the flat, the wings must be ready to rule if the pass is forward or backward.

Wing officials have responsibility for the passer if he scrambles past the line of scrimmage. If the quarterback is tackled out of bounds the wing official must rule on the legality of the contact. If the runner is driven out of bounds less than five yards past the scrimmage line, the covering wing official can handle the play and supervise players outside the sideline. When a play is more than a five-yard gain and the runner heads across the sideline, the covering wing official marks the spot while the referee or back judge escorts the players back to the field.

If the play ends beyond the line and in a side zone, the back judge should be the middle man in the V. The wing official tosses the ball to the back judge, who relays it to the umpire.

The back judge notes blocking ahead of the runner, or the runner himself if the runner should advance more than 10 yards downfield.

When a play is more than a five-yard gain and the runner heads across the sideline, the back judge should hustle out of bounds to protect players. On a play gaining considerably more than 10 yards, the wing official maintains the spot while the back judge escorts the players who went out of bounds back to the field.

The back judge is responsible for team B's goalline until the ball is snapped at or inside team B's 10 yardline; in that case, the back judge's starting position is on the endline.

On pass plays, the back judge must retreat far enough so he is always deeper than the deepest receiver. When the pass in flight, the back judge must quickly determine the intended receiver and get into the best possible position to observe the play. Both the offensive and defensive players must be observed for possible interference.

When a play ends inbounds near a sideline but a first down has been achieved, the covering official should give the stop-the-clock signal. It is not appropriate to give the wind-the-clock signal before the stop-the-clock signal if the play ended inbounds but a first down was achieved.

If the clock is to start on the ready signal, the covering official should indicate that to the referee by twirling the index finger. If the clock starts on the snap, the covering official crosses the wrists at waist level.

## Scrimmage Kicks

The referee must be ready to move in the appropriate direction in case of an errant snap or blocked kick. Once the kick is away, the referee takes a quick look to see the flight of the ball. If the kick is short and toward a sideline, the covering sideline official should be prepared to determine the spot the ball went out of bounds. If the kick is long and goes out of bounds, the covering official moves past where he thinks it flew out before walking toward the referee with his hand up — along the sideline — until the referee chops downward, telling him to halt.

If the receivers begin a return, the referee should move slowly downfield; if the runner breaks a long return, the referee may assume responsibility for the runner. The referee will get an inside-out look regardless of which sideline is involved since the appropriate wing official has sideline responsibility from endline to endline.

On blocked kicks, the referee should be ready to rule on the recovery and observe the advance of any player who runs with a recovered ball.

The umpire should move toward the line at the snap. Once the ball has been kicked and players from both teams have run past, the umpire pivots to the line judge's side. After the pivot, the umpire should move slowly downfield and observe action in front of the runner.

On a return to the middle of the field, the back judge has responsibility for the runner until the umpire takes the coverage; the point at which the transfer occurs depends on how far downfield the umpire has drifted after the kick.

The linesman observes the initial line charge and remains on the line until the kick crosses the neutral zone while the line judge releases on the snap and observes action on his side of the field between the neutral zone and the receivers.

On the vast majority of punts, however, both wing officials are responsible for their sideline from endline to endline and for covering the runner when the return is to their area. If the run is to the opposite sideline, clean up behind the play.

All deep receivers are the responsibility of the back judge. Once the ball is kicked, he judges the validity of any fair catch signal. The back judge has coverage responsibilities until the runner breaks into a side zone, when coverage transfers to the appropriate wing official. On a return to the middle of the field, the back judge has responsibility for the runner until the umpire takes the coverage; the point at which the transfer occurs depends on how far downfield the umpire has drifted after the kick.

The covering official, regardless of position, must beanbag the spot where the kick ends. That spot may be used for post-scrimmage kick penalty enforcement.

## Scoring Kicks

After the snap, the referee observes the actions of the kicker and holder. If the holder has to leave a kneeling position to catch or recover a poor snap, the referee must know whether the rules allow the holder to return to a kneeling position. After the kick, the referee is responsible for ruling on contact on the kicker and holder. If a kick try is blocked, the referee should blow his whistle immediately; a blocked field goal remains live, however.

In cases of a fake or a broken play, the referee assists on sideline coverage on the open side of the field.

Once he is confident the kicker and holder are in no danger of being roughed, the referee looks to the deep officials to learn the result of the kick. The signal should then be relayed to the pressbox.

The umpire should move toward the line at the snap, which will improve the view of the initial line charge and blocking.

If a blocked kick or fake results in a play toward the goalline on the line judge's side of the field, the umpire moves toward the goalline to assist on coverage of the runner. The umpire also helps rule whether or not a blocked kick crossed the neutral zone on his side of the field.

The wing official on the line of scrimmage (the one facing the referee when he is in position) will rule whether or not the kick crossed the neutral zone. If a pass is used on the fake, the wing must know if the passer was beyond the line. He can also help rule on ineligibles downfield on fake kicks that lead to passes. When a runner approaches the goalline, the wing on the line must be at the goalline to rule on the potential score.

The opposite wing and back judge stand beyond the end zone and behind the upright on their side of the field. The positioning can be adjusted once the ball is kicked to provide the best look possible. The wing is responsible for ruling whether the ball passed inside or outside the upright on his side; the back judge is responsible for ruling whether the ball passed inside or outside the upright on his side as well as whether the ball cleared the crossbar.

When a successful kick passes the upright or when the ball breaks the goalline plane and it is obvious it will not score, the back judge sounds his whistle and gives the appropriate signals. If the kick is blocked, is obviously short or the play turns out not to be a kick (fake or busted play), the deep officials should move along the endline and toward the nearest sideline.

# FREE KICK TO SIDE ZONE PART 1

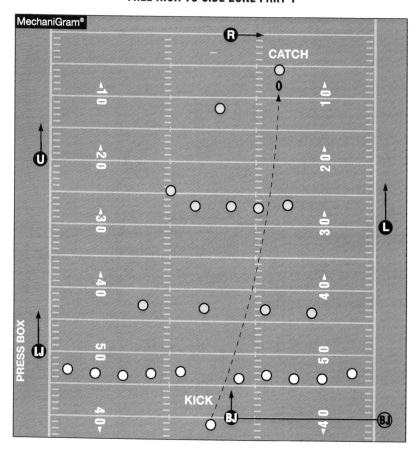

**Action on the field:** Receiver catches kick.

**Referee:** Observes catch. Signals clock to start when ball is caught by receiver. Moves to trail receiver and observes action of runner during return.

**Umpire:** Observes players in his area.

**Linesman:** Moves quickly upfield and observes action in his area.

**Line judge:** Watches for infractions involving free-kick line and contact involving players nearest him while moving upfield no farther than team R's 35 yardline.

**Back judge:** Watches for infractions involving free-kick line and contact involving players nearest him including kicker. Moves into field.

# FREE KICK TO SIDE ZONE PART 2

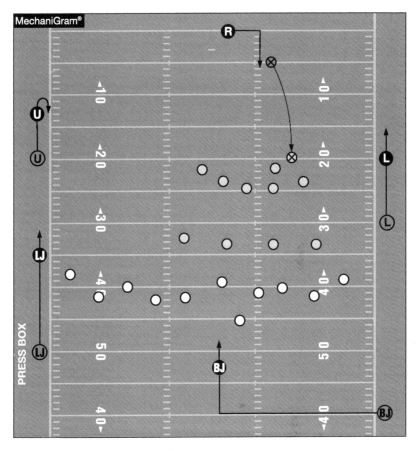

**Action on the field:** Runner advances.

**Referee:** Gives up coverage of runner to linesman. Observes action in front of runner (halo principle).

**Umpire:** Moves downfield with runner. Observes action in front of runner.

**Linesman:** Continues to move upfield. Takes coverage of runner when runner enters area.

**Line judge:** Observes action in front of runner.

**Back judge:** Observes action in front of runner. Goes no farther than team R's 45 yardline.

# FREE KICK TO SIDE ZONE PART 3

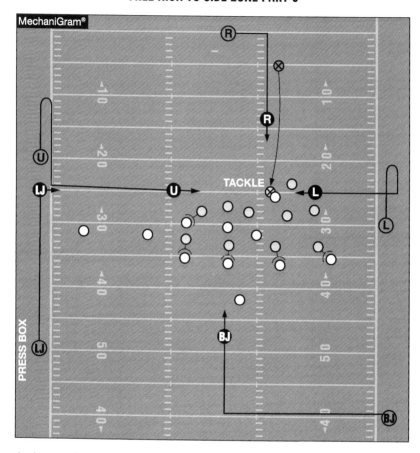

**Action on the field:** Runner continues advance and is downed.

**Referee:** Moves slowly downfield trailing runner. Observes players. When certain no penalty flags are down, signals new series for team R.

**Umpire:** Observes players. Mirrors spot until linesman marks progress. Moves to middle of the field and spots ball for next down.

**Linesman:** Observes players. Blows whistle and gives stop-the-clock signal when runner is downed. Squares off and holds spot. When referee signals possession for team R, instructs chain crew to set chains for new series.

**Line judge:** Observes players and hustles to spot.

**Back judge:** Observes players. Retrieves game ball from ball helper and relays to umpire. When referee signals possession for team R, moves into position for next down.

# FREE KICK OUT OF BOUNDS PART 1

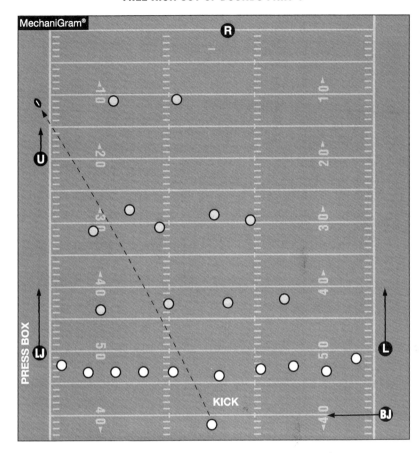

**Action on the field:** Ball kicked out of bounds in umpire's side zone.

**Referee:** Observes action in his area.

**Umpire:** Observes action in his area. Moves into position to judge which team caused kick to go out of bounds. Gives stop-the-clock signal when ball is out of bounds.

**Linesman:** Watches for infractions involving free-kick line and contact involving players nearest him.

**Line judge:** Watches for infractions involving free-kick line and contact involving players nearest him.

**Back judge:** Watches for infractions involving free-kick line and contact involving players nearest him including kicker.

# FREE KICK OUT OF BOUNDS PART 2

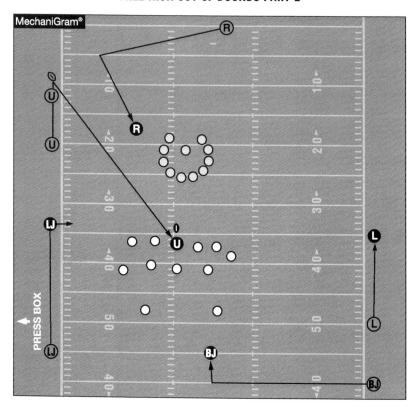

**Action on the field:** Team R chooses to take ball at its own 35 yardline.

**Referee:** Observes action in his area. Communicates with umpire to determine result of play. Obtains choice from team R. Signals team K's foul and points toward team R's 35 yardline, where ball will next be put in play. (If team R chooses a rekick, returns to position for rekick.)

**Umpire:** Observes action in his area. Communicates result of play to referee. Moves to hashmark at team R's 35 yardline to set ball for new series. (If team R chooses a rekick, returns to position for rekick.)

**Linesman:** Observes action in his area. Moves to team R's 35 yardline, where team R will begin new series, assists chain crew in setting chains. (If team R chooses a rekick, returns to position for rekick.)

**Line judge:** Observes action in his area. Moves to team R's 35 yardline, where new series will begin. (If team R chooses a rekick, returns to position for rekick.)

**Back judge:** Observes action in his area. Moves to position for start of new series. (If team R chooses a rekick, signals team K's foul, walks off penalty and returns to position for rekick.)

# FREE KICK OUT OF BOUNDS PART 3

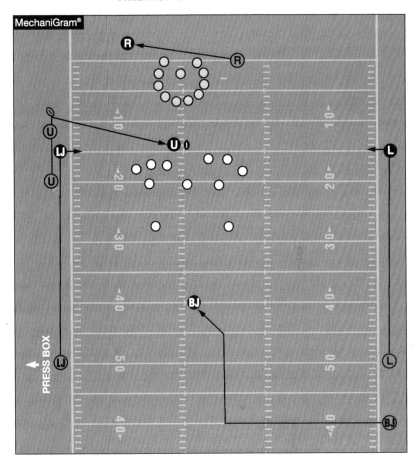

**Action on the field:** Team R caused the ball to go out of bounds.

**Referee:** Observes action in his area. Communicates with umpire to determine result of play. Signals new series will begin at spot where kick went out of bounds.

**Umpire:** Observes action in his area. Communicates result of play to referee. Moves to hashmark where new series will begin and sets ball.

**Linesman:** Observes action in his area. Moves to spot where new series will begin and assists chain crew in setting chains.

**Line judge:** Observes action in his area. Moves to spot where new series will begin. Holds spot until umpire sets ball for new series.

**Back judge:** Observes action in his area. Moves to position for start of new series.

# RUN UP THE MIDDLE PART 1

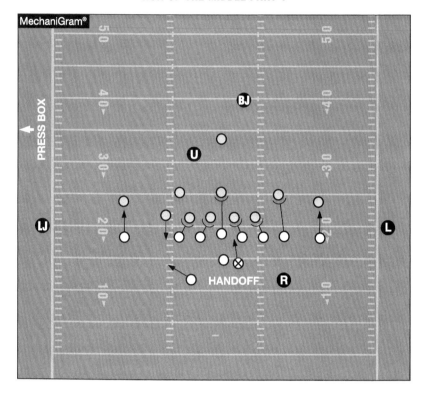

**Action on the field:** Handoff to a back.

**Referee:** Reads blocking of left tackle and reads run. Observes handoff and action around quarterback after handoff.

**Umpire:** Reads blocking of center and right guard and reads run. Determines point of attack and observes blocking there.

**Linesman:** Reads blocking of tight end and reads run. Observes blocking.

**Line judge:** Reads blocking of left tackle and reads run. Observes blocking.

**Back judge:** Reads blocking of tackle and reads run. Observes blocking.

# RUN UP THE MIDDLE PART 2

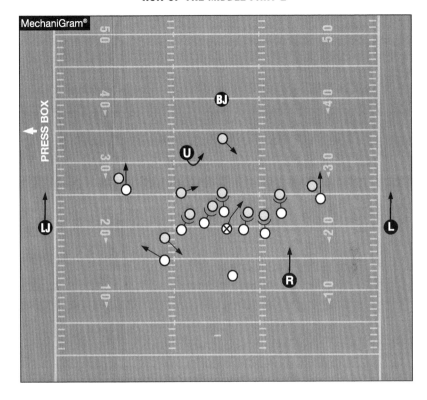

**Action on the field:** Runner advances.

**Referee:** Moves slowly downfield and observes action behind runner.

**Umpire:** Pivots to observe play. Observes action around runner.

**Linesman:** Moves slowly downfield and observes action in front of runner.

**Line judge:** Moves slowly downfield and observes action in front of runner.

**Back judge:** Observes action in front of runner.

# RUN UP THE MIDDLE PART 3

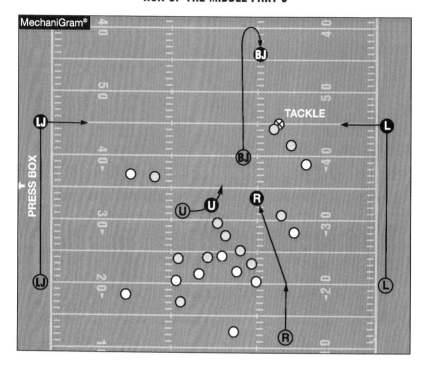

**Action on the field:** Runner continues advance and is downed.

**Referee:** Moves slowly downfield and observes players behind the ball in his area. If first down has been achieved and no penalty markers are down, signals linesman to have chain crew move the chains.

**Umpire:** Moves downfield and observes action behind runner. Observes players in his area.

**Linesman:** Moves quickly downfield and observes action around runner until runner enters back judge's coverage area. Observes players. Squares off to mark spot of forward progress. If first down has been achieved, gets signal from referee and instructs chain crew to move to spot. Assists chain crew in setting chains for new series.

**Line judge:** Observes action in front of runner on his side of the field. Squares off to mirror spot of forward progress. Observes players in his area.

**Back judge:** Observes blocking ahead of the runner and the runner himself if the runner advances more than 10 yards downfield. When runner is downed, observes players for dead-ball fouls.

# SWEEP TO LINESMAN'S SIDE PART 1

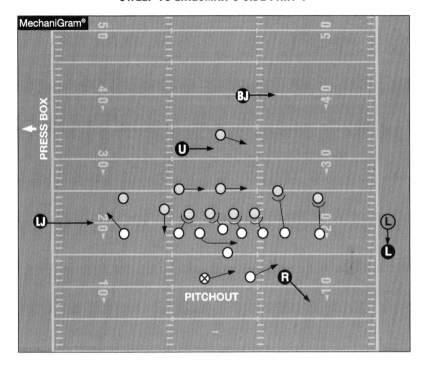

**Action on the field:** Pitchout to back.

**Referee:** Reads blocking of left tackle and reads run. Moves with flow of play. Observes runner and action around runner.

**Umpire:** Reads blocking of center and right guard and reads run. Determines point of attack and observes blocking there. Moves with flow of play. Observes blocking and action in front of runner.

**Linesman:** Looks through split end, reads blocking of tight end and reads run. As flow comes to his side, steps backward across sideline to prevent interfering with play. Waits until players have flowed downfield before moving to cover play. Observes blocking and action in front of runner.

**Line judge:** Looks through end, reads blocking of pulling left tackle and reads sweep to opposite side. Moves slowly toward play. Observes blocking and action of players not involved in flow of play.

**Back judge:** Observes blocking of tackle and reads run. Moves with flow of play. Observes blocking and action in front of runner.

# SWEEP TO LINESMAN'S SIDE PART 2

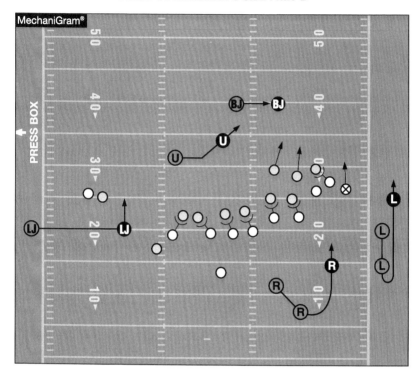

**Action on the field:** Runner advances.

**Referee:** Gives up coverage of runner to linesman. Moves slowly downfield trailing flow and cleans up after the play.

**Umpire:** Pivots and moves with flow of play. Observes blocking and action in front of runner.

**Linesman:** Takes coverage of runner and moves quickly up sideline, allow play to get past you-trail slightly. Observes runner and action around runner.

**Line judge:** Moves slowly downfield and cleans up after the play.

**Back judge:** Moves toward play. Observes blocking and action in front of runner.

# SWEEP TO LINESMAN'S SIDE PART 3

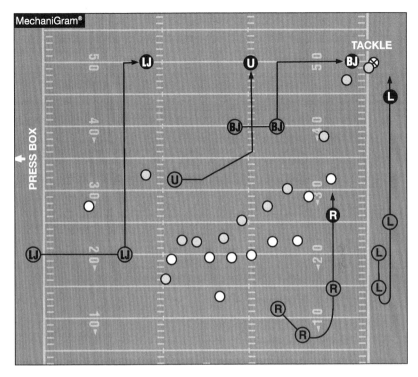

**Action on the field:** Runner continues advance and goes out of bounds.

**Referee:** Moves slowly downfield and observes players in front of the ball. If first down has been achieved and no penalty markers are down, signals linesman to have chain crew move the chains.

**Umpire:** Moves slowly downfield and observes players in front of the ball. Once spot is established, hustles to hashmark to set ball for next down.

**Linesman:** Gives up coverage of runner when runner enters back judge's coverage zone (halo principle). Moves down sideline and observes action behind the runner. Blows whistle and gives stop-the-clock signal when runner steps out of bounds. Hustles to dead-ball spot to prevent post-play action. If first down has been achieved, gets signal from referee and instructs chain crew to move to spot. Assists chain crew in setting chains for new series.

**Line judge:** Moves downfield with flow of play and cleans up after the play. Squares off to mirror spot of forward progress. Observes players in his area.

**Back judge:** Takes coverage of runner when runner enters coverage area (halo principle). Squares off to mark spot of forward progress. Observes players. Holds spot until umpire arrives to set ball for new series.

# DEEP PASS PART 1

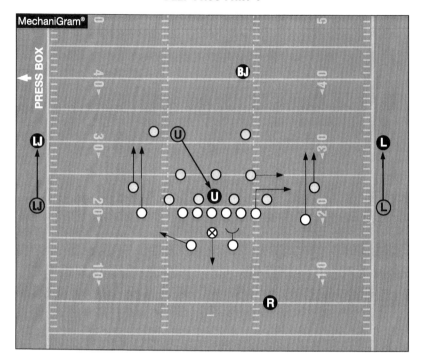

**Action on the field:** Quarterback drops back.

**Referee:** Keys on opposite-side tackle; reads pass when tackle retreats. As quarterback drops back, moves back to maintain distance between himself and quarterback. Observes blocking by backs.

**Umpire:** Observes presnap adjustments and legality of snap. Keys on center and guards; reads pass when linemen retreat. Steps up to the line of scrimmage and observes blocking.

**Linesman:** Identifies the eligible receivers on his side of the field. Uses extended arm signal to alert line judge that end is in offensive backfield. After snap, observes initial blocking, then moves slowly downfield and watches initial contact between receivers and defenders.

**Line judge:** Identifies the eligible receivers on his side of the field. After snap, observes initial blocking, then moves slowly downfield and watches initial contact between receivers and defenders.

**Back judge:** Observes tackle's block and reads pass, then shifts focus to split end. As receivers move downfield, moves back to maintain distance between himself and receivers. Watches initial contact between receivers and defenders.

# DEEP PASS PART 2

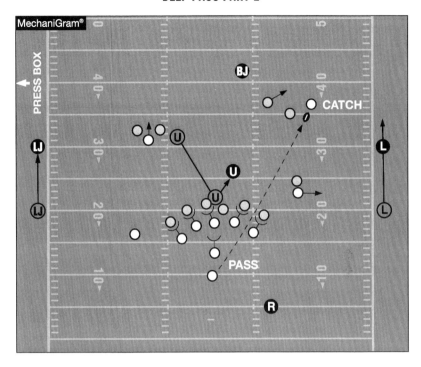

**Action on the field:** Pass thrown to and caught by receiver.

**Referee:** Observes passer. Moves downfield with flow of play.

**Umpire:** Pivots to follow flight and moves in direction of the ball.

**Linesman:** Moves downfield and maintains position about halfway between line of scrimmage and deepest receiver on his side, then moves quickly to get angle to observe attempted catch.

**Line judge:** Moves downfield and maintains position about halfway between line of scrimmage and deepest receiver on his side.

**Back judge:** Determines intended receiver and pivots to get angle and observe attempted catch.

# DEEP PASS PART 3

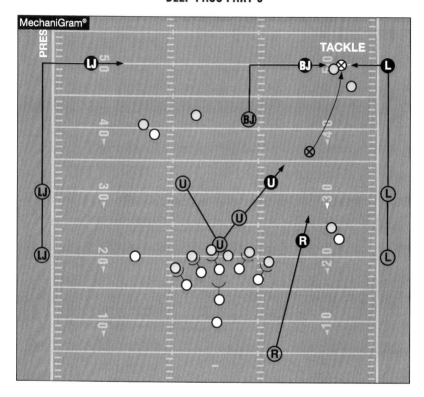

**Action on the field:** Runner advances and is downed.

**Referee:** Moves slowly downfield and observes players in front of the ball.

**Umpire:** Moves slowly downfield and observes players in front of the ball. Once spot is established, hustles to hashmark to set ball for next down.

**Linesman:** Continues to move downfield. Blows whistle when receiver is downed. Squares off to mark spot of forward progress. Stops clock if first down has been achieved.

**Line judge:** Moves downfield and observes players behind the ball in his area. Practices dead-ball officiating.

**Back judge:** Moves downfield and observes players in his area. Squares off to mark spot of forward progress. Echoes stop-the-clock signal if first down has been achieved.

# SCREEN OR PASS TO FLAT PART 1

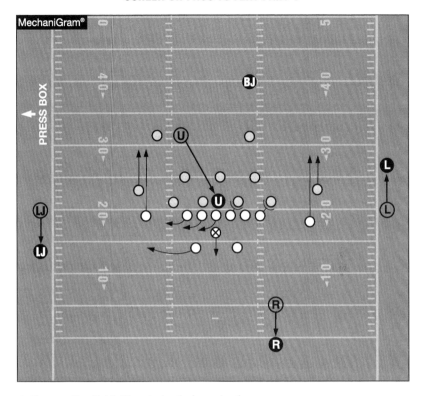

**Action on the field:** Quarterback drops back.

**Referee:** Keys on opposite-side tackle; reads screen or draw when tackle pulls. As quarterback drops back, moves back to maintain distance between himself and quarterback. Observes blocking by backs.

**Umpire:** Observes presnap adjustments and legality of snap. Keys on center and guards; reads screen or draw when linemen pull. Steps up to the line of scrimmage and observes blocking.

**Linesman:** Identifies the eligible receivers on his side of the field. Uses extended arm signal to alert line judge that end is in offensive backfield. After snap, observes initial blocking, then uses shuffle step to move slowly downfield. Watches initial contact between receivers and defenders.

**Line judge:** Identifies the eligible receivers on his side of the field. After snap, observes initial blocking; reads screen or draw when tackle pulls. Moves into offensive backfield to cover receiver out of backfield.

**Back judge:** Reads run when tackle fires out. Observes blocking by his keys.

# SCREEN OR PASS TO FLAT PART 2

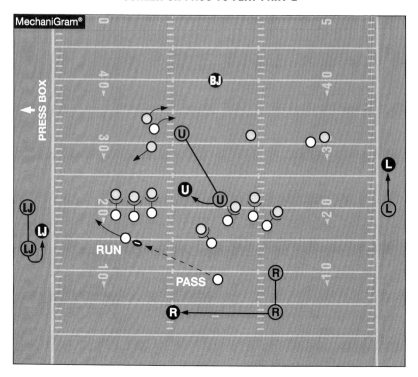

**Action on the field:** Pass thrown to and caught by back.

**Referee:** Observes passer. Looks to line judge for either backward pass signal, incomplete pass signal or no signal (complete forward pass). When passer is not longer threatened, moves to follow play.

**Umpire:** Observes blocking.

**Linesman:** Moves downfield and observes action of players in his area.

**Line judge:** Rules on whether pass is backward or forward. Observes action in front of runner.

**Back judge:** When position of ball is established, moves toward line judge's sideline and observes action in front of runner.

# SCREEN OR PASS TO FLAT PART 3

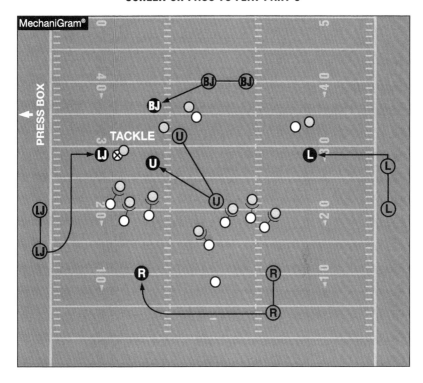

**Action on the field:** Runner advances and is downed.

**Referee:** Moves slowly downfield and observes players in his area.

**Umpire:** Pivots toward play and moves slowly downfield. Observes players in front of the ball. Moves to hashmark to set ball for next play.

**Linesman:** Moves downfield and observes players in his area. Squares off to mark spot of forward progress.

**Line judge:** Blows whistle when receiver is downed. Squares off to mark spot of forward progress. Stops clock if first down has been achieved.

**Back judge:** Moves toward play and observes players around pile.

# GOALLINE PLAYS: OFFENSE GOING IN PART 1

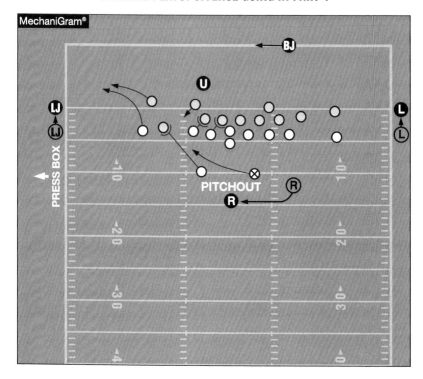

**Action on the field:** Pitchout to back, sweep left.

**Referee:** Reads blocking of left tackle and reads run. Moves with flow of play. Observes runner and action around runner.

**Umpire:** Reads blocking of center and right guard and reads run. Determines point of attack and observes blocking there. Moves with flow of play. Observes blocking and action in front of runner.

**Linesman:** Moves immediately to goalline at snap. Observes initial blocking.

**Line judge:** Moves immediately to goalline at snap. Observes initial blocking.

**Back judge:** Reads blocking of tight end and tackle and reads run. Moves with flow of play. Observes blocking and action in front of runner.

# GOALLINE PLAYS: OFFENSE GOING IN PART 2

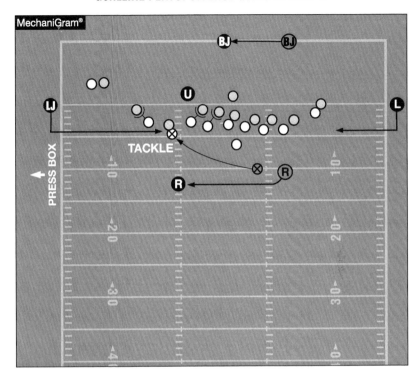

**Action on the field:** Runner stopped short of goalline.

**Referee:** Observes action.

**Umpire:** Observes blocking and action in front of runner.

**Linesman:** Officiates back to the ball and squares off to mirror line judge's spot.

**Line judge:** Officiates back to the ball to observe contact on runner and squares off to indicate forward progress. Blows whistle when runner is downed.

**Back judge:** Moves with flow of play and observes action.

# GOALLINE PLAYS: OFFENSE GOING IN PART 3

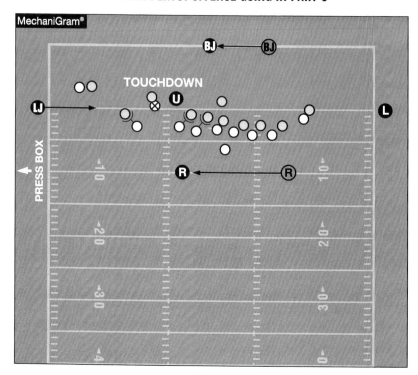

**Action on the field:** Runner scores.

**Referee:** Observes action. When line judge signals touchdown (if no flags are down), turns to pressbox and mirrors signal.

**Umpire:** Observes action.

**Linesman:** Observes action.

**Line judge:** Observes runner. When ball in possession of runner breaks plane of goalline, moves toward runner while straddling goalline, blows whistle and signals touchdown.

**Back judge:** Moves with flow of play and observes action.

# GOALLINE PLAYS: OFFENSE COMING OUT PART 1

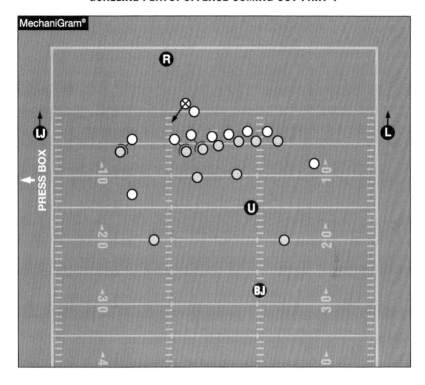

**Action on the field:** Handoff to running back.

**Referee:** Reads blocking of left tackle and reads run. Moves with flow of play. Observes runner and action around runner.

**Umpire:** Reads blocking of center and right guard and reads run. Determines point of attack and observes blocking there. Moves with flow of play. Observes blocking and action in front of runner.

**Linesman:** Moves immediately to goalline at snap. Observes initial blocking.

**Line judge:** Moves immediately to goalline at snap. Observes initial blocking.

**Back judge:** Reads blocking of tight end and tackle and reads run. Moves with flow of play. Observes blocking and action in front of runner.

# GOALLINE PLAYS: OFFENSE COMING OUT PART 2

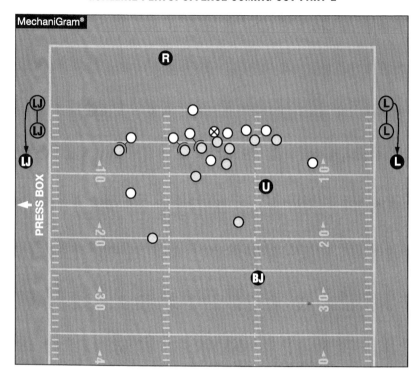

**Action on the field:** Runner advances beyond goalline.

**Referee:** Moves with flow of play. Observes runner and action around runner.

**Umpire:** Steps back to avoid interfering with play and pivots to observe play. Observes action around runner.

**Linesman:** Reverses field, moves with flow of play and observes action in front of runner.

**Line judge:** Reverses field, moves with flow of play and observes action in front of runner.

**Back judge:** Observes action in front of runner.

# GOALLINE PLAYS: OFFENSE COMING OUT PART 3

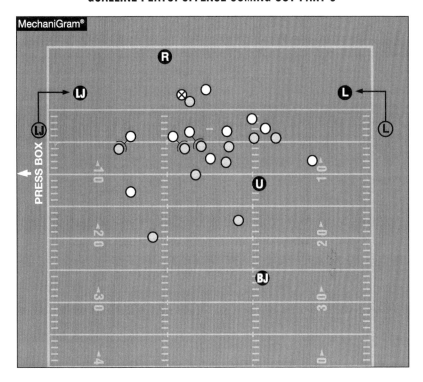

**Action on the field:** Runner downed in end zone.

**Referee:** Looks to appropriate wing official for progress spot or safety signal.

**Umpire:** Continues to observe blocking.

**Linesman:** If runner is clearly downed in end zone in coverage area, hustles in and signals safety. If runner is out of coverage area, hustles in for dead-ball officiating.

**Line judge:** If runner is clearly downed in end zone in coverage area, hustles in and signals safety. If runner is out of coverage area, hustles in for dead-ball officiating.

**Back judge:** Observes action of players away from pile.

# SCRIMMAGE KICK OUT OF BOUNDS PART 1

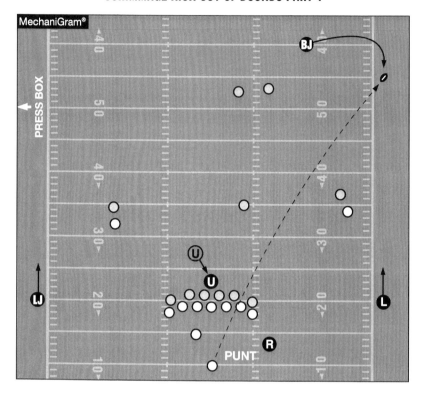

**Action on the field:** Ball kicked toward sideline.

**Referee:** Observes snap and action around kicker.

**Umpire:** Moves toward the line at the snap, observing initial charge of linemen and contact on the snapper.

**Linesman:** Observes initial line charge and remains on the line to rule whether or not the kick crossed the neutral zone. Moves quickly downfield when ball crosses neutral zone.

**Line judge:** Moves downfield on snap, observing action of players moving downfield.

**Back judge:** Observes receivers. Retreats to observe result of kick.

# SCRIMMAGE KICK OUT OF BOUNDS PART 2

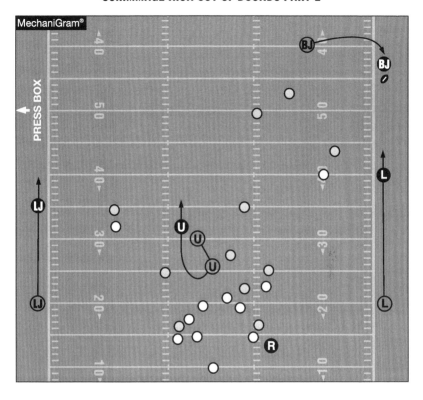

**Action on the field:** Kick is dead out of bounds.

**Referee:** Moves quickly toward sideline to observe flight of ball.

**Umpire:** Pivots toward the line judge's side of the field, observing players as they move downfield. Moves downfield on line judge's side of field.

**Linesman:** Moves down sideline. Observes action of players in front of ball.

**Line judge:** Moves down sideline. Observes action of players in front of ball.

**Back judge:** Gives stop-the-clock signal when he sees ball go out of bounds. Moves five to seven yards beyond spot where ball apparently went out of bounds, pivots and makes eye contact with referee.

# SCRIMMAGE KICK OUT OF BOUNDS PART 3

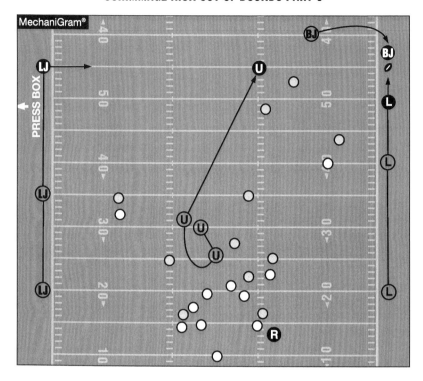

**Action on the field:** Ball spotted for new series.

**Referee:** With arm above head, observes back judge walking toward spot. When back judge reaches spot, drops arm with chopping motion. When certain there are no penalty markers down, signals linesman to move chain crew.

**Umpire:** Continues to move downfield and observes players. Moves to spot to set ball for new series.

**Linesman:** Hustles to dead-ball spot to prevent post-play action. Upon signal from referee, instructs chain crew to move to spot.

**Line judge:** Continues to move downfield and observes players. Squares off and mirrors back judge's spot.

**Back judge:** Walks slowly toward referee, stopping when referee drops arm with chopping motion. Signals first down for team R.

# SCRIMMAGE KICK TO BACK JUDGE'S SIDE ZONE PART 1

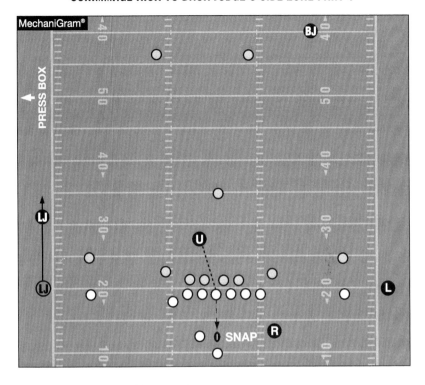

**Action on the field:** Ball snapped to punter.

**Referee:** Observes snap and action in front of and around kicker.

**Umpire:** Moves toward the line at the snap, observes initial line charge.

**Linesman:** Observes initial line charge and remains on the line to rule whether or not the kick crossed the neutral zone.

**Line judge:** Releases on snap and begins to move downfield, observes action on his side of the field between the neutral zone and the receivers.

**Back judge:** Observes action of receivers.

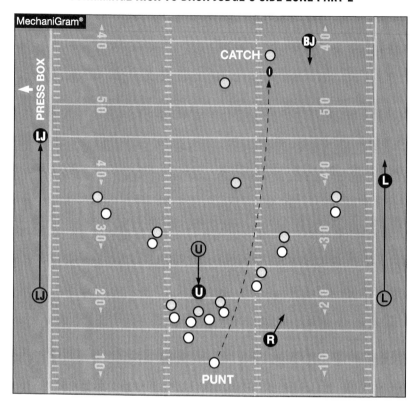

**Action on the field:** Receiver catches punt.

**Referee:** Observes line play after ball has cleared neutral zone. Moves slowly downfield.

**Umpire:** Pivots toward line judge's side of the field. Observes players as they move downfield. Moves downfield with flow of players.

**Linesman:** Observes action of players in front of ball.

**Line judge:** Observes action of players in front of ball.

**Back judge:** Drops beanbag at spot the kick ends. Moves with runner.

# SCRIMMAGE KICK TO BACK JUDGE'S SIDE ZONE PART 3

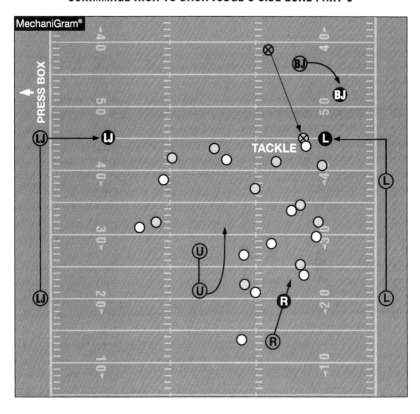

**Action on the field:** Runner advances and is downed.

**Referee:** Observes action of players. When certain there are no penalty markers down, signals linesman to move chain crew.

**Umpire:** Observes action of players. Moves to spot to set ball for new series.

**Linesman:** Takes coverage of runner when runner enters coverage area. When runner is downed, squares off to spot and stops the clock. Upon signal from referee, instructs chain crew to move to spot.

**Line judge:** Observes action of players. Squares off to mirror linesman's spot.

**Back judge:** Gives up coverage of runner when runner enters linesman's coverage area (halo principle). Observes action of players.

# SCORING KICK

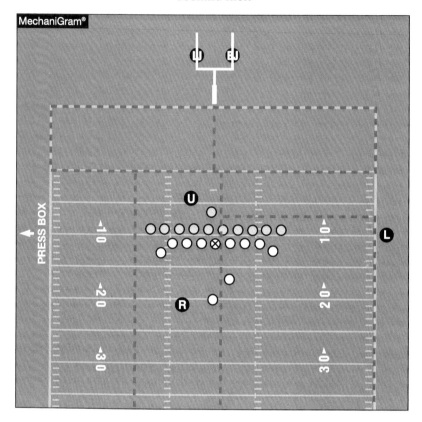

After the snap, the referee observes the actions of the kicker and holder. If the holder has to leave a kneeling position to catch or recover a poor snap, the referee must rule on the holder's ability to return to a kneeling position.

In cases of a fake or a broken play, the referee assists on sideline coverage on the open side of the field (the one vacated by either the line judge or linesman).

Once he is confident the kicker and holder are in no danger of being roughed, the referee looks to the deep officials to learn the result of the kick. The signal should then be relayed to the pressbox.

The umpire moves toward the line at the snap, which will improve the view of the initial line charge.

If a blocked kick or fake results in a play toward the goalline on open side of the field (the one vacated by either the line judge or linesman), the umpire moves toward the goalline to assist on coverage of the runner. The umpire also helps rule whether or not a blocked kick crossed the neutral zone on his side of the field.

Whether the linesman or line judge remains on the line or goes behind the goalposts depends on which side the referee lines up on. The wing official facing the referee remains on the line. The MechaniGram depicts a situation in which the linesman remains on the line.

On a blocked field goal attempt, the wing on the line will rule whether or not the kick crossed the neutral zone. That official also has sole responsibility for encroachment and rules on the legality of the snap.

If a pass is used on the fake, the wing must know if the passer was beyond the line. He can also help rule on ineligibles downfield on fake kicks that lead to passes. When a runner approaches the goalline, the wing must be at the goalline to rule on the potential score.

The wing can move toward the offensive and defensive linemen after the kick and use his voice to encourage players to unpile.

The back judge and wing official with him should confirm their ruling verbally before signaling, using "good" or "no, no, no."

The wing is responsible for ruling whether the ball passed inside or outside the upright on his side; the back judge is responsible for ruling whether the ball passed inside or outside the upright on his side as well as whether the ball cleared the crossbar.

When a successful kick passes the upright or when the ball breaks the goalline plane and it is obvious it will not score, the back judge sounds his whistle and gives the appropriate signals. If the kick is blocked, is obviously short or the play turns out not to be a kick (fake or busted play), the deep officials should move along the endline and toward the nearest sideline. Once the sideline has been reached, the deep official can move toward the goalline to assist on coverage of the runner.

CHAPTER SEVEN

# WORKING WITH THE CHAINS

Find out the names of the chain crew and ballboys, then call them by name when you need to communicate with them. Conversation between the linesman and chain crew during downtimes in the game can build a relationship that may prove helpful later.

**The** linesman's most important duty is to work with the line-to-gain equipment operators to ensure the down, the spot of the snap and the line-to-gain are tracked properly.

In common parlance, the device used to keep track of the downs and to mark the spot of the snap is called the box and the person in charge of it is the box man (granted, it could well be a box woman, box person or box kid). The apparatus consisting of two rods with 10 yards of chain between it is called the chains. The people in charge of the chains are usually referred to as the chain crew, or chain gang.

It is important for the linesman to have a thorough pregame meeting with the chain crew. He should introduce himself to the entire crew, thank them for their participation, get their names and write them on his game card. A complete review of responsibilities should be conducted with the chain crew and box man. Officials will often encounter a chain crew that "has been doing this for 30 years" and needs no instruction. In those cases, the linesman can remind the chain crew that not all crews do things the exact same way, thus creating the need for the meeting. Request they please bear with you while you review the required instructions.

If you think it's not important to instruct the chain crew, consider a court case that involved an NFL official.

During a preseason game in 1972, all-pro defensive end Charles "Bubba" Smith was at his post when a teammate intercepted a pass. At the end of the play, Smith found himself on the ground out of bounds, suffering from a serious knee injury. A lawsuit was brought against several parties, including head linesman Ed Marion and the individual who was holding the down marker, which Smith collided with upon going out of bounds.

The first trial of the case resulted in a mistrial due to the fact that the jurors could not agree on a unanimous verdict. The second trial resulted in a ruling in favor of the defendants. Of course, the NFL official was able to testify that he had instructed the chain crew in the proper methods of holding the stakes — or the outcome may have been different.

Since the Smith case, the physical requirements of the down marker and line-to-gain stakes have been changed for safety reasons, as has the placement of the chain crew during the down.

The case of Bubba Smith teaches that pregame responsibilities and sideline management are two of the cornerstones of risk management for officials — in any sport.

A four-person chain crew is preferable. If the crew consists of only three members, the person working the box can perform most of the duties involving the clip while the trail chain holder temporarily holds the box. It is recommended that the members of the crew wear distinctive vests or jackets furnished by home or game management. No one on the chain crew should double as a ball person or any other function.

The chain crew is part of the officiating crew and must remain impartial. If they are dressed in home team garb, not much can be done about it, but they should not be allowed to cheer or criticize the officials and must refrain from remarks relating to players and coaches and expressing

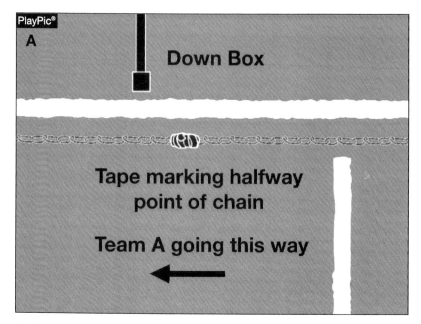

PlayPic®

A

Down Box

Tape marking halfway
point of chain

Team A going this way

←

The line to gain equipment should be positioned at least two yards off the field. The chain is on the field in the PlayPic for ease of reference.

opinions concerning any ruling or calls made by the officials. They are not to communicate with the visiting team and may not use cell phones or other electronic devices. That will avoid the impression that they are communicating information to the home team and ensure their attention will remain with their duties.

Any problems or situations the chain crew encounters while performing its job is to be brought to the linesman's attention. Remind the chain crew that you will resolve the situation, not them. If members of the chain crew are unable or unwilling to perform their duties, inform the referee. Either the game manager, the home team coach or the home team athletic director should also be alerted.

The chain should be taped at its midpoint. The tape helps determine if team A will achieve a first down on a five-yard penalty, thus precluding the need for a measurement. For instance, if the box is slightly beyond the tape, as in PlayPic A, the linesman can tell the referee, "It will be first down," or "Five will get you one." That can be indicated by a crew communication signal as seen in PlayPic B.

Conversely if the box is three links behind the tape and team B is flagged for a five-yard penalty, the linesman can check the tape and tell the referee, "They'll still be short."

If, during his pregame inspection of the chains, the linesman sees there is no tape on the chain, he should ask a trainer or team manager for a strip of tape about six inches long. The chain is folded in half and the tape wound

**This signal tells the referee that a five-yard penalty on team B will give team A a first down.**

around the links at the halfway mark. Some linesmen keep a roll of tape in their bag. In the locker room, a strip of tape is stuck under the bill of the hat. That can be used to tape the chain if necessary.

A zip tie can also be a lifesaver. If the chain breaks or the link holding the chain to the rod comes loose, the zip tie can provide a quick fix.

Ensure the stakes are equipped with safe, flat bottoms and check that the down box to confirm it operates correctly. Next the chain must be checked for length and integrity and that it is securely attached to the stakes and is free of kinks. The best place to check the length is between the 20 and 30 yardlines; that's where the ball will be placed after a touchback. If the chain is too long, the ball could be spotted beyond the 30 yardline and appear to be short of a first down. Both ends of the field should be checked. The examination may also reveal that the lines are not properly placed. Any corrections that are possible should be made.

## Procedures

When a first down is declared, the linesman goes to the sideline and marks the spot for the down marker holder with his downfield heel. The chains are then set according to the position of the box.

The chain is clipped along the sideline before it is moved off the sideline. Do not "eyeball" the intersecting yardline from two yards off the sideline.

The clip is placed at the rear-most edge of the rear-most five yardline, the yardline is set on the clip and the clip is never removed until the stakes

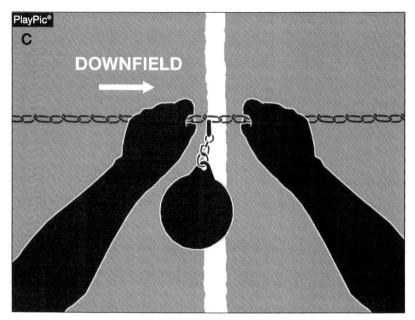

**DOWNFIELD**

Place the clip at the back edge of the first "big" line (e.g. 10 yardline, 25 yardline, etc.)

are in a new position, as seen in PlayPic C. The clip is a safety valve. If the chains are moved either in error or for safety reasons, the clip provides the exact chain location.

Once the clip is set, the box is moved six feet away from the sideline. The six-foot spacing allows the chain crew some cushion. The clip man should mark the new yardline with the second clip, leaving the original clip in place until after the first-down play ends. That's a backup in case the chains have to be returned to their previous position.

The trail stake goes immediately behind the box so the officials' view of the box is not obstructed. The lead stake holder is responsible to ensure the chain is taut at all times. When the trail stake is set behind the box, the trail stake holder should step firmly on the chain; that ensures the chain will be taut and that the trail stake will not be displaced when the lead stake is pulled. On long gains or after a change of possession, the linesman waits for the referee's signal before directing the chains to move.

All spots are taken from the forward point of the ball. The box holder is not to change the down or move the box until the linesman echoes the referee's announcement of the next down. Let the box holder know what signals will be used to tell the crew to stay put and to move. Many linesmen use the "stop" signal (arm outstretched, palm up and facing the chain crew) to indicate stay put and a beckoning motion of the hand or arm as the signal to move. A waving signal may be used to move the entire crew for a new series.

The linesman must memorize each line-to-gain. That eliminates the need to peek over his shoulder to check, which looks amateurish. It may take only a split second to look at the chains, but a punch or other foul could be missed even in that brief period of time. The line judge, looking across the field, can assist by informing the referee if the ball is beyond the line-to-gain; signaling and verbalizing the next down if the ball is clearly short, such as, "They're short"; or alerting the crew that a measurement may be needed by saying, "Freeze it! That's close!"

It is helpful if the box man is the first chain crew member at the new spot to assist with setting the chains. When he reaches the new spot he shall change the down on the box (old spot old down, new spot new down). A good technique is to have the box man echo the down to you after he relocates the box. That will let you know he has relocated and has the proper down shown on the box without you needing to look. The linesman should avoid looking at the box while players are moving into position.

Should the crew see a flag on the play, it is their job to hold their position regardless of any signal for them to move. If the linesman tells the crew to move, not seeing that a penalty marker is down, the crew should not hesitate to point out the flag to the linesman.

Whenever the goalline becomes the line-to-gain, only the box man is required. The linesman should provide a bean bag to the box man to be placed at the spot for reference in the event the box is removed. The chains are no longer needed and are to be laid down safely out of the way. On free kicks, the box and chains are not used. The chain crew should be positioned well out of bounds near the receiving team's 30 yardline.

Safety is paramount. If players approach, the chain crew must retreat and drop the equipment. That protects the players and the chain crew. The decision needs to be made early to reduce the possibility of injury. The chains and box are not to be carried away; they are to be dropped.

## End of a Quarter

At the end of the first and third quarters, the chains need to be moved to the opposite end of the field. The referee, umpire and linesman record the down, distance and clip position. The linesman uses a second clip to place on the chain where the box is. This can only be done when there are less than ten yards to go. He then grabs the chain with one hand on both sides of the clip, asks the stake holders to rotate so they are opposite of where they were when the quarter ended and then jog to the corresponding yardline on the other end of the field. To ensure that the chains are reversed, the linesman stands with his back to the field of play when first grasping the clip. When placing the clip at the new spot, he stands facing the field.

The linesman places the clip on the ground at the appropriate line, then asks both stakeholders to pull the ends taut. The box is placed once the umpire has set the ball. The line judge confirms the correct ball position with the umpire before he spots the ball.

If the quarter ends on a play which results in a first down, the chains and clip are set before the sides of the field are switched. That is seemingly unnecessary and takes a few minutes longer, but otherwise the double check on where the umpire places the ball is lost.

## Aiding Penalty Enforcement

If more than five yards are needed for a first down and the yardage for an accepted penalty may push the ball beyond the line-to-gain, the following procedure may be used. In a nutshell, it is merely temporarily moving the line-to-gain to reflect penalty enforcement, then measuring as usual.

For example, it's team A's ball, third and 12 from its own 21.5 yardline. A1 catches a pass and is downed at team B's 48 yardline. During A1's run, A2 held B3 at team A's 43.5 yardline. Before marking off the penalty, bring the chain onto the field alongside the spot from where the penalty will be enforced. Then, move the chain forward (toward team B's goalline) the exact number of yards specified by the penalty.

Next, note the location of the enforcement spot in relation to the front stake on chain. If the front stake is behind the enforcement spot, penalty yardage will net a first down. If that is the case, simply release the chain to go back to the sideline, step off the penalty and set the back stake of the chain on the nose of the ball at the new succeeding spot.

On the other hand, if the front stake is in advance of the enforcement spot, penalty enforcement will not produce a first down. If the flag in the play cited is short of the front stake, the referee should pinch the chain at the spot adjacent to the flag. Next, while the referee continues to pinch the chain, the linesman repositions the clip at the yardline where it was at the start of the down (in the above scenario, that's team A's 25 yardline) and along the inbounds line closest to the enforcement spot. Then the referee should place the nose of the ball at the spot where he is pinching the chain.

For team B fouls, use the identical procedure, except bring the chain onto the field alongside the enforcement spot and set the clip backward (toward team A's goalline) the exact number of yards specified by the penalty for team B's foul.

CHAPTER EIGHT

# TIMEOUTS

Either a player or the head coach may request a timeout. In the event the head coach is ejected, he may designate an assistant to perform that function. The head coach's designee shall remain in place for the entire game except in case of emergency.

**Any** official should grant a valid timeout request and immediately stop the clock if it is running. That official reports the timeout to the referee. The referee indicates the timeout by repeating the stop-the-clock signal and indicating the team being charged the timeout by facing the team and extending both arms shoulder high, giving three "chucks" in that team's direction.

All officials must record the number and team of the player requesting the timeout, the quarter and the time remaining on the game clock. Each official then confirms with the referee the number of timeouts each team has remaining. The linesman and line judge inform the coaches on their respective sidelines of the timeouts remaining.

The back judge is responsible for timing the timeout. The one-minute count begins when the referee is informed of the timeout. When 45 seconds have expired, the back judge sounds his whistle twice so the linesman and line judge can inform their teams. When the minute has expired, the referee whistles the ball ready for play.

The procedure for signaling an official's timeout is the same as for a charged timeout. After stopping the clock, the referee has the option of tapping his chest to indicate it is an official's timeout. Play should resume as quickly as possible.

If the official's timeout is for injury, any team conference must be an "Outside Nine Yard Mark Conference" if approved by the referee.

During timeouts, wing officials are responsible for monitoring conferences near your sideline. Help get players promptly back onto the field.

## TIMEOUT WITH BOTH TEAMS AT THE SIDELINES

During the timeout, the referee and back judge remain in their positions in the offensive and defensive backfield respectively, the umpire stands over the ball and the linesman and line judge should take positions midway between the ball and their respective sidelines.

# TIMEOUT WITH ONE OR BOTH COACHES ON THE FIELD

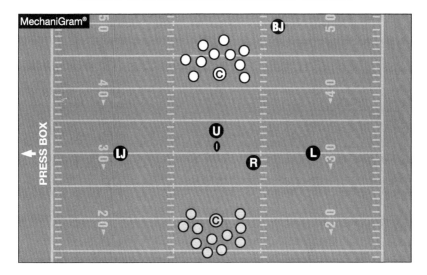

During the timeout, the referee and back judge remain in their positions in the offensive and defensive backfield respectively, the umpire stands over the ball and the linesman and line judge should take positions midway between the ball and their respective sidelines.

## INJURY TIMEOUT

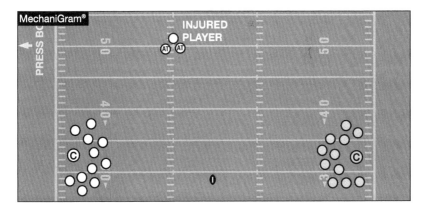

When an injury occurs and the referee grants an authorized conference, it must be an "outside the nine-yard marks conference." That conference provides an opportunity for players to get water. If the injured player is between the hashmarks and the numbers, the team whose sideline is affected should move away from the injured player.

# CHAPTER NINE

# MEASUREMENTS

One area in which a football crew can shine involves measurements. A well-handled measurement ensures that a team is properly rewarded for a good offensive or defensive effort.

**When** the referee calls for a measurement, the linesman should have the box moved behind the lead stake. That is a reference point in case the line to gain should somehow become lost during the process. As the chains are being brought onto the field, the line judge should use his foot to indicate the intersection of the five yardline where the chain is clipped and a line through the ball parallel to the sideline. That is the spot where the linesman will place the clipped part of the chain.

The linesman brings the chain in from the sideline with the chain crew members. Putting one hand on the links on each side of the clip improves the linesman's chances of keeping track of the proper link in case the clip falls off the chain. The clip must be placed on the back edge of the line for the measurement. A good double-check is for the linesman to state that the next down will be first if the ball is beyond the stake or the next down of the series if it is short. (Example: "It will either be first or fourth.")

Depending on which team has the ball, the back judge or line judge can obtain another game ball from the offensive team's ball helper. If the back judge has the ball, he can toss it to the line judge before the measurement.

The back judge holds the ball in place from the downfield side (the side of the ball opposite from the sideline the chains are coming from). Once the linesman tells the referee he has the chain on the proper mark, the umpire takes the forward stake from the chain crew member, then pulls the stake to ensure the chain is taut. The referee rules whether or not the ball is beyond the front stake.

## First Down

If the measurement results in the award of a new series, the referee signals the first down. The linesman need not hold the chain as he accompanies the chain crew back to the sideline, but he must go all the way to the sideline and indicate to the chain crew where the new series will begin.

If the measurement occurred in a side zone, the back judge should remain with the ball on the ground as a double-check to ensure the ball is spotted properly for the next play.

Whether or not the result is a first down, the referee must wait for the linesman's signal that the chain crew is back in position before giving the ready-for-play signal.

## Short of a First Down

If the measurement is in a side zone and does not result in a first down, the umpire should keep control of the stake. The referee uses his hands (or thumb and index finger if the ball is inches short of the front stake) to inform both benches how short the play ended of a first down (see PlayPic, next page).

The back judge continues to hold the ball in place. The referee grasps the chain at the link in front of the ball and rises. The referee should grasp the chain with two hands with the link that will be used to place the ball

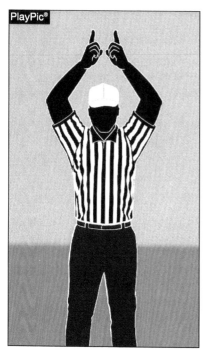

between his hands; that will ensure the proper link is maintained. The back judge continues to hold the ball in place. Referee, umpire, line judge and linesman walk to the nearest hashmark. The spare ball (the one the line judge is holding) is then placed at the proper spot.

Once the ball is placed, the back judge may remove the ball that was used in the measurement and return it to the ball helper.

If the measurement occurred on fourth down and team A is short, the referee signals the change of possession by giving the first down signal toward team A's goalline. The referee then sets the ball in the same position as it was when it became dead so its foremost point becomes the rear point when the direction is changed. The new rear stake is then moved to the new foremost point of the ball.

# MEASUREMENT IN SIDE ZONE OPPOSITE THE CHAINS

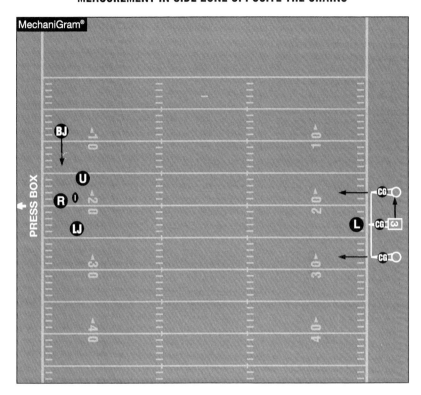

**Action on the field:** Play ends in side zone close to a first down.

**Referee:** Stops clock after seeing that measurement is necessary. Waits at spot for arrival of chain gang.

**Umpire:** Waits at spot for arrival of chain gang.

**Linesman:** Has box holder move box behind lead stake. Brings chain in from sideline with chain gang members to spot indicated by line judge.

**Line judge:** Indicates intersection of the five yardline where chain is clipped and line through ball parallel to sideline with beanbag or foot.

**Back judge:** Moves to spot to hold ball in place on ground.

# SHORT OF A FIRST DOWN PART 1

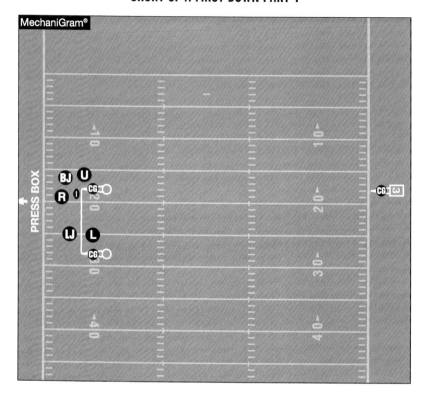

**Action on the field:** Team A is short of a first down.

**Referee:** Rules whether or not ball is beyond front stake. Uses hands or fingers to inform both benches how short the play ended of first down.

**Umpire:** Holds lead stake.

**Linesman:** Holds chain in place.

**Line judge:** Gets spare ball from ball helper.

**Back judge:** Holds ball in place on ground.

# SHORT OF A FIRST DOWN PART 2

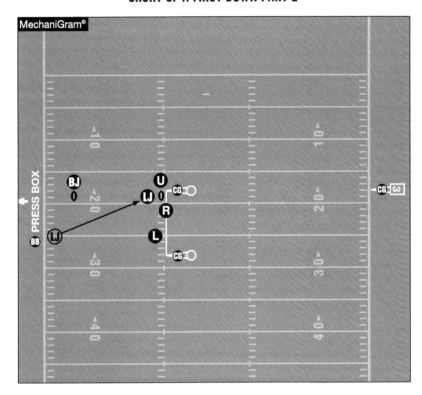

**Action on the field:** Chains are moved to hashmark for ball placement.

**Referee:** Grasps chain at link in front of ball and rises. Walks to nearest hashmark. Gets ball from line judge and places it. Waits for linesman's signal that chain gang is back in position and other officials are ready before giving ready-for-play signal.

**Umpire:** Maintains control of front stake and walks to nearest hashmark.

**Linesman:** Maintains control of clip and walks to nearest hashmark. Accompanies chain gang back to sideline and sets chains for next down.

**Line judge:** Delivers ball to referee for placement.

**Back judge:** Holds ball in place on ground.

# TEAM A AWARDED A FIRST DOWN

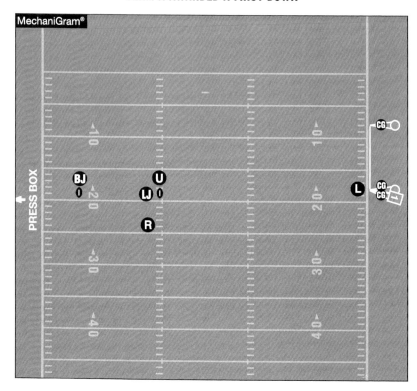

**Action on the field:** Team A is awarded a new series.

**Referee:** Signals first down. Waits for linesman's signal that chain gang is back in position and other officials are ready before giving ready-for-play signal.

**Umpire:** Moves to hashmark where ball will next be snapped. Gets ball from line judge and places it.

**Linesman:** Returns to sideline with chain gang and indicates where new series will begin.

**Line judge:** Delivers ball to umpire for placement.

**Back judge:** Holds ball in place on ground.

# CHAPTER TEN

# WORKING THE SIDELINE

"We don't mind a coach stepping out on the field between plays to call a play or for instructions, but when the ball is going to be snapped they need to be back behind the limit lines."

— Mike Fitch, executive director of the Texas Association of Sports Officials

**Not** everyone is cut out to be a wing official. Linesmen and line judges have to make tough judgment calls at the sideline as well as between the sidelines. They are intimately involved in every play, be it a run or a pass. And then there are the coaches, who are constantly in the official's ear (and sometimes his face, too).

It takes patience, diplomacy, a keen eye and often a deaf ear to work the wings.

There are two facets to sideline work. One is communication. The other is ensuring that no one gets in your while you're covering a play, which colloquially is known as keeping a clean sideline.

Great linesmen and line judges excel at both aspects. Here are some reminders about those two vital parts of the job.

## Communication

Wings must be people-oriented. While wings cannot (and most often should not) respond to every comment, wisecrack or complaint, the lines of communication cannot be totally shut down.

Most coaches identify communication as the single most important attribute of an official. Knowing when not to communicate is as important as knowing what and when to have a dialogue with a coach.

Allowed. The head coach is entitled to an explanation of all unusual rulings or situations. The explanation will normally be given by the wing official, but may be given directly by the referee as necessary. The emphasis is that communication is with the head coach only. A timeout is not charged for those types of discussions. Officials' timeouts to talk to coaches outside of a coach-referee conference should seldom be allowed. Officials can talk with coaches during a dead-ball period.

The head coach may request the aforementioned conference at any time while the ball is dead. The purpose of the rule is to review a possible misapplication of a rule by the officials, not to question a judgment call, nor to express an opinion on the quality of the calls.

Additionally, a head coach may expect to have reasonable and brief questions answered by the wing official. The head coach is entitled to the following information for all fouls:

- The nature of the foul (e.g. holding, personal foul, etc.).
- A brief description of the act.
- The number or position of the offending player.
- The enforcement and the result of the enforcement.

For example: "Coach, your number 62 was called for holding. He pulled down an opponent. The penalty is 10 yards from the spot of the foul and second down will be repeated."

Under no circumstances should a number be fabricated. If that player wasn't on the field (or worse yet, that number is not assigned), credibility has just been destroyed.

Stating the offending player's position instead of the number is acceptable, as in, "The motion man cut up too soon." But, "Everybody but the center moved" may sound smart alecky.

Not allowed. Assistant coaches and other authorized sideline personnel (athletic directors, chain crew, photographers, ball boys, athletic trainers, security personnel, etc.) are not entitled to any information from the officials. However, the wing official may opt to respond to simple, direct questions, such as the number of the down or the number of timeouts remaining.

Coaches are not supposed to make any remarks regarding the officials' behavior or judgment. They do not have an expressed or implied right to scream at or berate officials. Brief exclamations such as "Oh, no!" or "That wasn't interference," or requests like, "Can you watch for holding on number 65?" are acceptable, but comments such as, "They are holding on every play," "Call it both ways," "This is the worst officiated game I've ever seen," etc., are not acceptable.

A warning (not a sideline warning) may be given for the first offense. Any subsequent violations should be treated as unsportsmanlike conduct.

Depending on the severity or harshness of the accusations, an unsportsmanlike foul or an ejection could be appropriate for a first offense. Warnings should not be given for any statement by anyone along the sideline that involves direct criticism of an official or an official's decision. Those remarks usually include the word "You." Such statements must result in an immediate unsportsmanlike conduct foul. Gestures such as hands to the throat, suggesting the official "choked," must be dealt with harshly.

Any visual depiction of a foul such as tugging on a shirt is an immediate foul. A team should not be penalized for actions by anyone for whom the head coach is not responsible (such as photographers). Simply ask the game administrator to remove the offender from the sideline.

Profanity. There is no clear consensus on the use of foul language. The rules prohibit profanity and vulgar language; however, opinions vary as to what words are vulgar or profane. Some will argue that "damn" is profane; others will find any word acceptable dependent on the context in which it is used. An example is the so-called F-bomb, which is one of the most versatile words in the English language. It serves as a noun, transitive verb, intransitive verb, adverb, adjective and exclamation. It is the latter form that may be very well ignored. A coach who sees his wide-open receiver drop a pass and exclaims "Aw f- - -" might be excused by many officials. However, almost any other use of the word will elicit a flag.

An old bromide is that language that is unacceptable in class is verboten on the field. However, we should recognize that as a far-fetched analogy.

Because of the wide disparity in personal preferences, crews should find common ground on the acceptability of foul language so the game is officiated consistently.

## Ears Open

Active, effective listening by officials is part of good communication. A good listener tries to understand thoroughly what the other person is saying. In the end he may disagree sharply, but before he disagrees, he wants to know exactly what is being discussed. It's important to listen carefully to coaches and ask pertinent questions to find out exactly what is on their mind. Treat them as a valued customer when they think they have a problem.

Officials should communicate in a calm manner and should not say anything except to answer a question. There must be no profanity of any kind. It is also not a good idea to try using humor in a confrontation.

## Sideline Interference

Prior to 1989, wing officials had a lot of company on the sideline. That's because coaches, substitutes, athletic trainers — even spectators — often watched the game from the proverbial best seat in the house: just outside the field of play.

The NFHS made sideline control a point of emphasis from 1984-88. Included in the 1988 rulebook was the following passage: "It is imperative that management restrain people or have monitors to keep all sideline personnel to a minimum and as far back from the sidelines as conditions allow. … It is important that cheerleaders, mascots booster club personnel, etc., be kept away from the playing area."

For four years starting in 1984, the Wisconsin Interscholastic Athletic Association experimented with a rule that limited the number of people who could be outside the team box and between the sideline (the restricted area). Iowa and Arizona also used the rule on a test basis in 1988. All three state associations were pleased with the results. Sideline conduct improved and congestion was alleviated.

A rule change proposed in 1989 was adopted: Only three coaches were allowed between the team box and sideline.

But that only addressed part of the problem. Those three people in the restricted area still got in the way of officials, as seen in MechaniGram A. In 2009, the rule was given more teeth. Three coaches could occupy the restricted area but had to retreat to the team box when the ball was live. The first time in a game the rule was violated, the team received a warning. The second time, a five-yard penalty for delay of game was enforced. A third infringement led to a 15-yard penalty. If a team were foolish enough to draw a fourth flag, the result was a 15-yard penalty and ejection of the head coach.

Yet another tweak to the rule occurred in 2010. A distinction was drawn between a non-

If a non-player is in the restricted area while the ball is live, a sideline warning is issued.

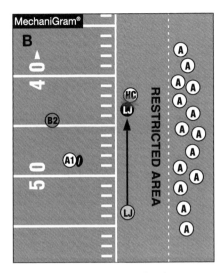

**It is a foul if there is unintentional contact with a non-player in the restricted area.**

player being in the restricted area during a live ball, and accidental contact between an official and someone in the restricted area (MechaniGram B). The latter is treated as a personal foul with a 15-yard penalty. A second such foul resulted in 15 yards and ejection of the head coach.

Note that any of the above situations is treated as a dead-ball foul. The penalty is enforced from the succeeding spot and does not negate the play.

A violation of one rule does not affect the penalty for the other rule. Thus if in the initial incident, there is contact and in a subsequent incident, a team member is observed in the restricted area while the ball is live and it is the first non-contact violation, the penalty is still a warning. The fact a 15-yard penalty was enforced for the contact foul does not affect the penalty sequence for non-contact violations of the restricted area or the team box.

The rules are sound but too many officials turn a blind eye to violations. Some officials believe that if a coach is strictly doing his job and not berating the officials or interfering with the game, no foul should be called. That puts the safety of players, non-players and officials in jeopardy. Not to mention the possible legal ramifications.

To brush up on the rules involving the sideline, review these caseplays:

**Play 1:** B1 intercepts a pass and advances to team A's 40 yardline. During the run the wing official unintentionally runs into (a) team A's assistant coach in the restricted area at team B's 45 yardline, or (b) team A's head coach who's on the field at the 50 yardline. **Ruling 1:** In (a) and (b) team A's head coach is assessed a 15-yard non-player, illegal personal contact penalty at the succeeding spot. A second offense would result in a disqualification of the head coach.

**Play 2:** B1 intercepts a pass and returns it for a touchdown. During the run, the wing official must veer off to avoid contact with team B's assistant coach, who is in team B's restricted area. The covering official drops his flag near team B's restricted area. Also during the run, team B's head coach leaves the team box and runs along the sideline but out of bounds all the way to the goalline. **Ruling 2:** Team B has committed two separate non-player fouls. Team B's assistant coach is guilty of being in the restricted area while the ball is live. The head coach has fouled by being outside his team box. Because non-player fouls by the same team cannot be combined to create a multiple foul, the penalties for both fouls are administered. Team B is issued a team warning and is penalized five yards. Team A may choose to have the yardage penalty enforced on the try or the subsequent kickoff.

**Play 3:** In the first quarter, the assistant coach for team A accidentally collides with an official who is covering a play. Team A is penalized 15 yards for illegal personal contact by a non-player. In the second quarter, while a play is in progress, an official observes an assistant in the restricted area. **Ruling 3:** The coach being out of the team box brings the first warning for team A for violation of the restricted area. There is no yardage penalty. The personal contact foul and the violation of the restricted area are not combined.

**Play 4:** In the first quarter, team A's coach is out of the team box when he accidentally bumps an official. Team A is penalized 15 yards. In the second quarter, the same coach is penalized 15 yards for unsportsmanlike conduct. **Ruling 4:** The coach is not ejected. Contact without a coach outside the team box is not combined with the foul for unsportsmanlike conduct to create an ejection.

**Play 5:** A1 is illegally in motion at the snap. Team B's coach is out of the team box when he accidentally bumps an official. **Ruling 5:** The penalty for team A's motion foul is enforced. The penalty for team B's foul for a coach outside of the team box is a non-player foul and is therefore penalized as a dead-ball foul, even though the contact occurred during a live ball.

# FINAL CHECKLIST

☐ It is impossible to sum up the duties and responsibilities of the wing officials in just a few words. But the following list provides some key points that separate the great wings from the average ones.

☐ Keep your head on a swivel, making a visual sweep of players to watch for dead-ball fouls. Don't "officiate air." Always keep your eye on players.

☐ Do not go around or jump over players to mark progress. Move into the field until you approach players, then stop.

☐ Always begin a play with your feet behind the sideline. Once the play begins, establish a cushion and maintain it during the play. You want to observe the play, not be part of it.

☐ When the ball is snapped inside team B's five yardline, the wings break to the goalline at the snap and officiate back to the ball, if necessary.

☐ In the matter of keys, in a balanced formation, strength is always considered to be on the line judge's side. The back judge keys on the widest receiver

☐ The wings have to follow receivers downfield but should look back to see if a passer is truly setting up to pass. On quick passes in the flat, the wings must be ready to rule if the pass is forward or backward.

# FREE FOOTBALL RESOURCES FROM REFEREE.COM

Referee.com is the #1 destination for FREE downloadable guides, online quizzes, and digital content for officials at all levels.

## GET A FREE ISSUE OF REFEREE MAGAZINE